Are You in a Caregiving Relationship and Don't Know It?

Finding a Balance of Loving and Caring

Wendy Packer, R.N.
Linda J. Parker

Printed in the United States of America
ISBN-13: 978-1463507497
ISBN-10: 1463507496
Library of Congress Cataloging-in-Publication Data
    Packer, Wendy.
    Parker, Linda J.
    Are You in a Caregiving Relationship and Don't Know It?

Cover design by Paige Ragan

DEDICATION

At the top of my list, my husband Dr. Paul R. Packer, the best diagnostician and caregiver related to all things medical or not. Samantha and Rebecca, my beautiful daughters who are so accomplished in all that they do. My sweet grandchildren Calista and Eli, tangible joy and love bugs ... I love you beyond the beyond. My beloved parents ... my first caregivers ... you are always with me. To "glorious" Ellie who has become a "second mother" to me in so many ways ... I cherish you. And last but not least, Charlie ... my handsome Shih Tzu who fills me up with unconditional love!

--WP

CONTENTS

"The best and most beautiful things in the world cannot be seen or even touched—they must be felt with the heart."

Helen Keller

FOREWORD BY MR. ELDERCARE: MARTIN R. SABEL

Whether you are a caregiver now or know someone who is, you're about to open a refreshing, new window on your life. When you finish reading *Are You in A Caregiving Relationship and Don't Know It?* you'll never look at the role of caring for another person the same way again.

I know because it happened to me ... and caught me completely by surprise in the process!

Linda and Wendy approach defining caregiving in a way I've not seen elsewhere. This book is both subtle and thought provoking. It's written from a deep well of love and understanding about people, particularly the "hidden army" of family caregivers doing the heroes work of caring for a child, spouse or parent.

It's refreshing, eye-opening, and heart opening at the same time.

As an elder care strategist, senior advocate, author and caregiver myself, I thought I understood caregiving inside out. After all, families call on me to guide them through one of life's most difficult passages. My book, *The Elder Care Survival Guide: How To Care For Elderly Parents Without Losing Your Money, Your Family or Your Mind*, covers all aspect of caregiving – from dealing with family to finding help to paying for care to managing stress. Plus I've consulted with thousands of families.

So I'm an expert, right?

Well, yes and no. Yes, when it comes to advising others; not necessarily, when it's my own family.

When it's your family, all the professional distance and objectivity that comes with being emotionally detached from a situation, tends to go out the window.

I started reading the book early one Tuesday morning. Since my mom at age 89 is now in a nursing home, my day was fairly typical. I see Mom multiple times every week.

That day I visited with again, checked with the nurses about her medications and progress in physical therapy, and picked up her dirty clothes to wash. All in all, that a fairly typical day for me. All in all, I was feeling pretty good about myself.

That evening and again the next day, I continued reading. Late the next afternoon, I get a call on my cell. It's mom. "Martin, where have you been? I haven't seen you. I need your help."

Her dementia wouldn't let her remember our visit the day before nor be specific about what help she needed. All she knew is she wanted to see me.

I knew there was nothing wrong. She was lonely and wanted company.

Frankly, it irritated me.

Yes, I know caregivers are not "supposed" to get upset or angry. Heck, I'm the professional. I'm the last person who should suffer from negative emotions! Right? I only wish it were that way.

The truth is that all caregivers sooner or later run into that same reality. I have a job; have a wife, a son, a daughter, and a life. Any family member who takes on the responsibility of balancing another person's life with your own understands that frustration is a normal by-product of the plate spinning we all do as caregivers.

It's part of the territory.

Since my brother, aunt and niece had been to visit mom that day I knew she was well. She had lots of social interaction with family and friends. I was tired from a very busy day at work. I wanted a break. I felt an emotional knot tightening around me. Should I go or not? What will my family think? What if something really IS wrong?

Resentment began sneaking into my heart. So did guilt and shame. I didn't like the way I was feeling but it was there.

Without me thinking much about it, one of Wendy's remarkable insights popped into my head. A comment about stabilizing self-care and selflessness solved the dilemma. That's what I enjoy about this book. As you read, Wendy and Linda are planting little seeds of strength and common sense that can blossom into life-changing ideas.

I met Linda when she was teaching at a webinar for book writers. She was supportive of my desire to write what later became, *The Elder Care Survival Guide: How To Care For Aging Parents Without Losing Your Money, Your Family or Your Mind!* At the time, I had no idea she had firsthand experience providing care for a special needs daughter.

Like most caregivers, she had no idea she was a caregiver until she met Wendy. As she points out in her introduction, "Having a child with special needs hadn't seemed extraordinary—it just happens to be my life." That view changed when she met Wendy Packer.

Wendy has a knack for changing the way people look at life.

She is one of those once-in-a-lifetime people you meet who you never forget. She lifts you up spiritually, emotionally, and energetically. She shares that in this wonderful, loved filled book. She is one of those "natural" caregivers who draws strength from helping others. You'll find yourself drawing strength for her through her written words.

From her experience grew *Are You in A Caregiving Relationship and Don't Know It?* Her message of how important it is to love and care for yourself as a caregiver is one I wholeheartedly support. It's an important message that most caregivers ignore at their peril.

Linda and Wendy, both extraordinary caregivers, wonderful writers, and amazing individuals bring a new dimension to understanding the driving force behind caregiving. You will discover a number of unique insights into the way love and care intersects and interacts.

As you do, Wendy will change the way you look at your role as a caregiver and you'll be the better for it.

Martin R. Sabel, "Mr. Elder Care"

Author, *The Eldercare Survival Guide*
www.eldercare1.com

FROM THE AUTHORS ... Wendy

Have you ever had an epiphany regarding your life, an awakening, or rebirth that truly set your life path in a new direction for your benefit as well as for others? People wear many hats in their life juggling this and that, which can be detrimental as well as beneficial. I've always heard "you do too much" or "you can't do everything." "Why is that?" I would ask and the response was always the same "something has to give, no one is perfect."

Those words finally made an impact in my life. It was at that moment in time that my epiphany became my reality ... I became my mother's caregiver.

Care giving was nothing new to me. I was a caregiver at 6 years of age. That's right, at six years old I was helping my Mom take care of my paternal grandmother. This was the start of my caregiver career.

I say career because that's what I've done and presently do. I've taken care of family, patients, children, parents, clients and grandchildren. One would think, since I was the caregiver "extraordinaire," I could handle anything and everything that came my way. But that wasn't the case regarding my mom; I fell into the caregiver trap. I was so consumed with my caregiver responsibilities that I lost myself in the process.

It has been said, "War is a series of catastrophes which result in victory," thus, this book was born.

Love… isn't that what makes the world go round? Yes, it is and so much more. When one thinks love, caring enters into the equation as well. Those two words go hand-in-hand.

Our book was written with love, infinite love. It will transform caregivers' lives. Just allow yourself to absorb our caring guidance and you will truly understand the message for all caregivers. The message of how important it is to love and care about yourself. Caregivers must care for themselves as well as the person they are taking care of.

I thank Linda, the "ultimate caregiver" for all of her guidance, support, tenacity and most of all her immense love regarding this wonderful caring project.

Love and Light,
Wendy

FROM THE AUTHORS ... Linda

I had been in the role of caregiver for some twenty-five years—without ever even realizing it. At a conference in New Mexico several years ago, I was seated next to a woman I had never met.

During breaks and sometimes when we shouldn't have been chatting at all, we began to share with each other about our lives and our families. After telling her about my daughters, one of whom has special needs, she said to me, "Oh, then you are a fulltime caregiver."

Her words startled me—I almost corrected her. And then I realized, *hummm ... I guess I am.*

Since that fact seemed to me to be something I *should* know, I tried not to act too surprised. Yet for me, it was a revelation. I thought of myself as being much like any other mother. Having a child with special needs hadn't seemed extraordinary—it just happens to be my life.

After mulling over my 'new' label, I began to realize that it fit. I also realized that there must be millions of other people who act as caregivers every day without ever realizing they are doing something special.

Did my new insight change anything? Well, no, it certainly didn't change my situation, but it did alter my perception of it. I began to cut my daughter—and myself—more slack when we dealt with things in unconventional ways. I started to be prouder of both of us for the way we handle life in general. I even started accepting more help when it was offered.

Writing this book with Wendy, who is by calling a giver of light, brightness, healing and care, has been both a blessing and an emotional process. The more we read, researched, and talked to caregivers, the more we realized many of them, if not most, are struggling.

While there are certainly stories of joy, there are far more stories of sadness, exhaustion, and brokenness. *It all comes down to a matter of love* ... love for the people for whom you provide care. Love for yourself as the extraordinary creation you are. And love for others who are struggling in their role of caregiver or care recipient.

If this book does only one thing for those who read it, I pray that it will open a window in their lives to allow the light of love to shine through, even if at first, it comes through only as a tiny glimmer. Thank you Wendy for allowing me be part of this message, and to all who read the book, thank you for opening your heart to its simple and timeless message of love.

Blessings,

Linda

ACKNOWLEDGEMENTS

To Elsom Eldridge Jr., for all his guidance and knowledge; after all he is the "Obvious Expert." Dr. Dwight Damon, President of the National Guild of Hypnotists the largest international hypnosis organization in the world. While attending the NGH Annual 2009 Convention and Educational Conference this book became my dream while presenting a workshop on "How to be the Expert in Taking Care of the Caregiver." Lastly, to supportive friends and colleagues, who are ultimate caregivers … making the world such a beautiful place.

Love is just a word until someone comes along and gives it meaning.

Anonymous

TO ALL THE CAREGIVERS

The word caregiver, as you will discover in this book, has many meanings and even more implications. While it is our goal that this book will help you see caregiving in new and different ways, it is never our intention to diminish or minimize the role of the many dedicated individuals who give of themselves, providing care, attention, and of course, love, to others in need.

By caregiving for ill, injured, or aging family members and loved ones, caregivers face often-unrelenting demands and responsibilities of enormous weight. These quiet heroes deserve the utmost respect from all of us.

"The most important thing in life is to learn how to give out love, and to let it come in."

Morrie Schwartz

1 LIFE BEGINS WITH CAREGIVING ... LOVE IS OPTIONAL

Your life began at the mercy of a caregiver. For nine months, or some approximation thereof, your first caregiver provided for your needs.

Your biological mother might have been fourteen, alone and terrified, or forty and thrilled, annoyed, or just amazed you showed up at all. She may have centered her days around you, focusing on anything she might consume, acquire, avoid or abandon, purely for your benefit alone. And then again, she may have tied a leather strap around her arm, and thought of your wellbeing only in a moment that passed without acknowledgement, just before a dirty needle entered her vein.

You survived in your dark, liquid, prenatal existence because your first caregiver made a sufficient number of necessary choices to keep your tiny being alive. Whether the process involved adoration or ambivalence, she provided what you needed for your development into a puzzled and wrinkled infant who blinked, cried, and openly objected to your unceremonious launching into the world.

Maybe you adore her today; maybe you avoid her. Perhaps you never met her. Whatever the situation, this woman—*your biological mother*—was your first caregiver in life, and without her, you would never have existed at all.

How inevitable is the heartbreak when a lover who longs to hear the words "I love you" hears "I care about you" instead? Two simple words "love" and "care," and as difficult as it is to describe the complex feelings they each represent, most people have a clear understanding of the distinction between the two.

Love stirs within people amazing depths of strength, courage, hope and endurance. Lifetimes are devoted to the pursuit of love. *Love me; love me more; love me truer; love me more passionately; unconditionally and forever*—love to the max becomes a quest. Moreover, people tend to look for this 'optimal love' from not just one person, but in all of their love-based relationships, whether it is familial, romantic, or platonic love.

Ask people to define the word "lover" and they will tell you about someone who is passionate and adoring. But ask them to define the word "caregiver" and it becomes another story entirely. Now they talk about a selfless person changing diapers for a senior citizen. Although dictionaries remind us to expand the definition of caregiver to include anyone, paid or volunteer, who attends to a child or dependant adult, the core message is clear. Being a lover is an intimate, personal involvement while being a caregiver may be an unselfish devotion or it may be nothing more than a paycheck at the end of the week, but either way, society tells us it falls far short of the love relationship.

Many 'volunteer' caregivers will say that their role in providing care is not a job they would have taken had it been emotionally acceptable or financially feasible for them to do otherwise. They are caregivers, not by choice, but by default. And in the ultimate irony, being a caregiver does not actually require you to care about the person you *care for*.

How does this happen? Since caregiving is so integral to our life journey, why is love sometimes so starkly absent from the role yet in other situations serves as the motivating force that fuels the caregiver? More personally for you, what could it mean in your life if you are able to add the positive qualities of a loving relationship to your role as caregiver and the benefits of caregiving to your love-based relationships?

Your life-journey began in the hands of a caregiver. Chances are it will end the same way. Regardless of the path you travel through this world you will likely give and receive love, but you will most assuredly give and receive care. While the two words really ought to be interchangeable, life will remind you over and over again in the most painful of ways that they typically are not.

But it doesn't all have to be a negative experience. You cannot always change who you will be in caregiving or care receiving associations with, but you can make tremendous changes in how you interact within these relationships. Likewise, you can transform your loving relationships in meaningful and lastingly beneficial ways by making the very best aspects of caregiving a part of them.

When you think about it, why wouldn't you want to do this? Being in a caregiver relationship is not something limited to Aunt Susan who gave up her career to take care of Grandma. If you have parents, children, siblings, lovers, a spouse, a boss, employees, clients, or friends, you are going to be in caregiver/care receiver relationships of varying types and degrees. Who we love and when we love can be random and spontaneous, but caregiving is both a deliberate decision and an inescapable reality of life on this earth.

Love may make the world go round, but compassionate caregiving and care receiving provides the real anchor that keeps us from spinning off into outer space.

2 CAREGIVERS VS. LOVE GIVERS

"I love you."

"I love my job."

"I love the New York Yankees."

"I love horseradish."

A wide range isn't it? We throw that word around every day, describing our passion for an out-of-this-world homerun, a song just released by a past runner-up on American Idol, or the French fries from a diner that recognizes the sanctity of always using fresh peanut oil in the deep fryer.

And as casually as we give the word away, we also horde it and calculate its use. Be sure you say, "I love you," to your friend or family member just before he boards the plane—*you never know*, we tell ourselves. Always say the three magic words to our children, our siblings and our parents, just in case our actions have left any room for doubt.

Lovers carefully strategize who first says, "I love you" in a romantic relationship. These rules are very clear; say it too soon and you look vulnerable and needy, hold out too long and you seem distant or shallow.

Some husbands, especially those from the days when men 'were men' were known to limit the use of the words "I love you" even to their wives and children. Envision a Clint Eastwood movie character on horseback telling his wife, "I said it twenty years ago when we got married. There's no need to repeat it; I'll let you know if anything changes." And with a tip of his hat, Eastwood rides off to the next gunfight, cattle drive, or barroom brawl leaving his spouse to draw her own conclusions as she watches him and his stallion become a distant speck on the horizon.

Most wives today would haul this cowboy into divorce court, claiming alienation of affection. ...*even if he looked like a young Clint Eastwood.*

Love is Subjective

From your spouse to your job to the New York Yankees and horseradish, love is subjective and very complex for most people to understand. Love means to you whatever it means to you, and to your spouse or partner, whatever it means to him or her. And it is possible, even likely, that neither of you fully knows what the meaning is.

Even in parent-child relationships, motherly love or a father's love is not the same thing from one parent to the next. Love is so important to us we spend a lifetime trying to gain it and keep it. Love is also so ill-defined we fill counseling sessions and divorce courts with the reality that two people can differ vastly in what they each believe love to mean.

We all have our own unique ways of measuring love, of testing love and of grading it. Need proof?

Ask your significant other to write a list of ten things he or she does to show love to you and ten things you do that makes him or her feel loved by you. Make your own list as well. First, note both the disparity between the two lists and the overlaps. Now go back and circle everything on either list that qualifies as an act of caregiving by your definition.

The overlaps are critical. They indicate ways that the two of you love each other and the message of loving is getting through so that both parties feel it. But the uncircled items are the real indicator of your relationship; hopefully they form a very, very short list. Love may show up with a racing heartbeat and a feeling of breathlessness, but love sticks around when it helps do the dishes, pay the bills, and remembers to pick up the dry cleaning. We want love.

But we need and require care.

Love is All We Have ... Or Maybe Not

Euripides said, "Love is all we have, the only way we can help the other." Perhaps what he really meant is, "Love is all we have, the only way we can care about each other."

Love shows up in our lives wearing many hats. If we actually sat down and tried to sort out the hats, we'd find some bare heads missing a hat and some empty hats without heads. Love is headgear. Sometimes a headdress to show off to others; sometimes a helmet to protect us; and sometimes a hood behind which we hide. Love offers protection, serves as a signal to the world that we are valued by someone else, and can be as sporty or as fashionable as we desire—a Stetson, an Indiana Jones, a fedora, or a Kentucky Derby hat covered in red silk roses.

Putting on the 'love hat' feels good because it's sexy, elegant and flashy all at the same time. My parents love me; the prom queen or high school quarterback loves me; the man or woman of my dreams loves me. But love without caring will leave us watching our cowboy (or cowgirl) ride into the sunset, while we stand by, holding our hat in our hands.

No matter how beautiful our hat, peacock feathers and all, if it is not well seated on our heads, the first strong gust of wind will knock it off. Scramble, and you may be able to catch it, but if the hat is too flimsy or the wind too strong, it will be carried out of our reach, sailing along on the wind, coming to rest at the feet of someone else.

Caring, on the other hand, is a deliberate and thought-driven process. Unlike love, that seems to catch us by surprise, we care for others because we have thought it over and have made the decision that we want to invest our time and energy in that person.

Sometimes we make the investment because of how much we love the person involved. Sometimes we make it because money motivates us, while other times the nagging motivator of guilt compels us. The degree to which we invest measures our level of caring. The reason we invest measures our heart.

The goal is to put on the most appealing love 'hat' and then secure it with hatpins, a chinstrap or whatever it takes to keep it securely in place. The goal is to love the people we care about and to care about the people we love.

A Simple, but Countercultural Idea

Melding together love and caring begins when we open ourselves to the possibility of embracing a new outlook on what love means, what caring means, and what we honestly seek in relationships. Remember, love is what we want. Caregiving is what we need and what we inevitably, in one form or another, wind up giving to others throughout our lives.

In your quest to live your best life possible, you can follow the path that so many others before you have taken, experiencing life through the eyes of your resentments, hurts, self-limiting fears and idealistic, unrealistic expectations. You can search for perfect love that reads like a movie script and smells like a bottle of expensive perfume. Or you can open your heart and your mind to loving on a deeper, higher and more lasting level—the kind of loving that happens when you allow caring and loving to become one and the same.

Countercultural ... yes. But counterintuitive ... *surely not.* According to recent marriage and divorce data compiled by the CDC, [i] 7.1 percent (per thousand) of the people in America get married each year while the divorce rate annually is whopping 3.5 percent per thousand. Does your intuition tell you to play those odds?

The combination of things that people do and choose to not do in the effort to make their marriages and love relationships work statistically doesn't have a proven track record of turning out very well. With a divorce rate that is nearly half the marriage rate, all of us have plenty of reason to question many of the world's established perceptions and understandings about love.

Getting married or entering into long-term relationships isn't supposed to be a serial process for repeat offenders—at least we don't assume it will be each time we try it. When people advise others to "try, try again until you get it right," they are usually not suggesting running through a string of relationships with other people. And considering we spend our childhood and teenage years trying to build, grow or repair relationships with our parents, friends, siblings, teachers, bosses, coaches and others, why do we sometimes get to adulthood so poorly prepared to succeed in loving relationships? Perhaps it is simply because we incorrectly try to compartmentalize loving and caring as different—and separate—experiences.

Start at the Beginning

Parents come in all skill levels. Some are great, most are adequate, and the law should and sometimes does stop other parents from ever getting near children again. However, the *really good* parents are identified by only two qualities: they both love their children and care for their children. At times, they make decisions that are not the best and sometimes they make decisions that are flat-out wrong. But in general, as long as they are acting with loving intentions and in caring ways, they pass the test as good parents. The better they are able to keep the two in balance, loving as much as they care and caring as much as they love, the greater success they have as a parent.

Young children tend to interact with many people who are in caregiving roles. In addition to their parents, they may have babysitters, child minders, nannies, or childcare providers in their lives. They may receive care from some or all of the following people: grandparents, step parents, older siblings, neighbors, friends, relatives, playgroups, nursery school workers, preschool teachers, Kindergarten teachers, teachers aides, coaches, ballet instructors, music teachers, afterschool workers, summer camp or day camp workers, church school teachers, pediatricians, the family doctor, nurses, nurse practitioners, dentists, speech therapists, medical specialists from any target area where they are receiving individual attention, and others who may have been omitted from this list.

Wow.

That's quite a long inventory and one that is important to fully process. A caregiver can be a full time job or it can be someone with whom a child only interacts briefly. The action involved, not the duration or frequency of the action, establishes the act of caregiving. A dental hygienist who cleans a child's teeth is caregiving to that child, even if the interaction only occurs for twenty minutes, twice a year.

Developing an awareness of the types of caregiving received by children (and of the people who provide it) is helpful because your childhood experience as a care recipient provided critical groundwork for your own caregiving skills. We tend to model as adults what we experienced as a child. Even adults who start out with strong intentions not to replicate the mistakes of their parents often repeat the negative practices of a poor caregiving parent with their own children.

Sometimes when the childhood experience was negative, the person will seek new models to emulate for parenting, which is precisely the reason that Dr. Phil, Oprah, and other advice experts find the market so receptive to what they have to offer. And the fortunate twist is that in some situations, the presence of even one positive caregiver in a child's life can have a powerful impact, overshadowing other poor caregivers, *even though the good example is not the child's primary caregiver.*

A teacher, coach, older sibling or any other caregiver who acts with compassion sometimes counterbalances and even outweighs a poor parental caregiver in terms of imprinting a child with a sense of self-worth and an understanding of what it genuinely means to both receive love and care and give love and care. Knowing this makes the roles of the millions of adults who provide caregiving to children *extremely* important and reinforces for all of us that learning to combine both love and caring may be the most critical life lesson any of us can master.

So Is It Caregiving or Love?

If, at this point, there is still a question in your mind as to whether this is a book about love, romance, relationships, and platonic love or is a book about caregiving and care receiving in times of need, the answer is simple. It's both.

Neither love nor care has a very strong history of being able to survive in a healthy and sustainable way without the presence of the other. You want one, you need the other, and your greatest chance of attaining both comes in learning to recognize the difference in the two and knowing how and when to give and receive them in a combo-package throughout your life, while consistently looking out for the needs of your number one caregiving responsibility—*yourself.*

"There are only four kinds of people in this world: those who have been caregivers; those who currently are caregivers; those who will be caregivers; and those who will need caregivers."

Rosalynn Carter quoting a colleague in the field of caregiving

3 WHEN CHILDREN BECOME CAREGIVERS

We don't always think of children as caregivers, yet the reality of how often they fall into this role may surprise you. You may also be surprised as you realize the subtle ways a child might be manipulated into the role of caregiving without the child or even the adult realizing it has happened.

Children, as we all believe, are supposed to learn, laugh, play and make mistakes along the way. Adults are in charge, making sound and reasonable decisions while living their lives as reliable and responsible people. Children receive care. Adults give care.

Really? Who are we kidding to think that this sometimes doesn't get turned upside down?

More than five years ago, the National Alliance, together with the United Hospital Fund, issued one of the most comprehensive studies on the subject of children as caregivers. At that time, over 1.4 million children between the ages of 8 and 18 provided care for a sick or disabled parent, and these findings were limited to the U.S. alone. What that number has risen to in recent years or how large it is on a global basis is challenging to estimate as children may serve in caregiving roles without there ever being documentary evidence of their actions.

Who can accurately keep tabs on how many children provide care to other siblings, a parent who is injured or ill, a grandparent, or any other disabled family member? Adults receiving care from a child are often reluctant or embarrassed to discuss their caregiving situation and in some cases, may not even be cognizant of the extent to which they are requiring care and impacting the child's life.

It's Not All Bad News

Children wind up as caregivers for any number of reasons, some bad, some inexcusable and some unavoidable. But let's start with the acknowledgement that being a child in the role of caregiver is not always a negative experience.

The child who spends his afterschool time watching television may benefit from the downtime, but he or she isn't exactly 'better off' than a child, who while acting as a caregiver, takes on new responsibilities, grows in compassion and patience, and perhaps even gains valuable life skills.

The types of roles a child may play as a caregiver are as varied and diverse as those a caregiving adult may assume. Studies of caregiving children show that over seventy percent of these children are assisting a grandparent who lives in the home with them (or spends considerable time in the home) or they are caregiving for a parent. In roughly eleven percent of the cases, the care recipient is a sibling of the caregiving child.

For a child, the first life-changing/life-disrupting element of caregiving often involves relocation. Sometimes a family moves into the home with the grandparent, but more often, the grandparent moves in with the son or daughter and the grandchildren. This change alone is considerable to children and often requires them to give up a portion of their personal space as the family appropriates rooms or beds for the household's newest member.

Even when a child is not directly involved in the caregiving, the differences it makes in his parent's lives to act as caregiver for their own parent, and the changes it makes in the household in general, have a direct impact on the child. The strangled and struggling economy is further complicating this situation. A study conducted by the National Alliance for Caregiving and Evercare found that since 2009, financial pressures have caused one in every five caregivers to give up his or her own residence and relocate into the home with the person for whom he provides care.

In some cultures, the multigenerational household is still common, just as it used to be in the U.S. Catch a rerun of *The Waltons* and you get an instant lesson in the evolving cultural anthropology of America. Although life in days past was never as idealistic as "Goodnight John-Boy" made it seem, there have always been valid benefits to multiple generations living in a single household.

Three generations under one roof creates natural opportunities both for grandparents to help with childcare and for children to take part in caregiving for the grandparents. But because most families in the U.S. are no longer structured this way, and there are often now many complex relationships of stepchild/stepparents and half-siblings, the lines of responsibilities are blurry and overstretched geographically. When illness or aging makes it necessary to merge households, the change becomes disruptive and stressful simply because it is change.

Grandpa may need help because arthritis has limited his mobility, but that doesn't mean that he can't be his grandson's favorite chess opponent and spinner of tall tales. In many ways how heavily the responsibilities of caregiving weigh upon a child has to do with (1.) the degree to which these responsibilities define a child's life and (2.) how much the care recipient is able to communicate love and appreciation for the child's caregiving efforts.

If children can act as caregivers by being runners, picker-uppers, helpers, assistants and companions, and still have time to participate in sports, hobbies and generally goof-off, then there is little to suggest that being a part-time caregiver is a problem, especially in an atmosphere that is warm, pleasant, and reassuring. But what happens to a child when the 'atmosphere' is a sickroom that smells like a stale bedpan?

Surprisingly, the child caregiver may still be just fine. If a child is able to get past any discomfort he or she feels about the idea of an illness or infirmity, then natural curiosity often takes over. A child's willingness to ask the questions an adult might never ask, such as, "Does it hurt when you put on your artificial leg?" often puts him or her in a position to gain valuable insights that an adult caregiver could easily miss.

Kids are generally pretty curious about bodily functions. They are often still figuring out things about how their own bodies work. Because they are not so very far removed from experiencing certain fears like that of wetting your pants in public, children can be among the most compassionate of caregivers. A child's inquisitiveness can even make some aspects of caregiving that repel adults feel like a science project to the young caregiver.

In Katie Maxwell's book, *Bedside Manners*, she writes about ways adults can interact with children who are ill. Her insights however, are equally useful when viewing the roles in reverse. Maxwell describes children between the ages of six and nine, saying:

"They have a penchant for details and facts. They begin to ask How and Why questions … Using their own past experiences and collection of limited facts, they begin to come up with conclusions on their own rather than relying on what adults tell them to be true."

Not only are children sometimes more comfortable with illness or disability than adults are, children also have an advantage over adults when it comes to understanding one of the interrelated issues of caregiving; that of dependency.

Feeling dependent on others is often a source of anxiety for people during illness or injury. Children relate to fears about being able to take care of yourself, support yourself, and survive on your own. Most children either have had these fears themselves or have at least considered the possibilities. They fully understand and are especially sensitive to the vulnerable feelings associated with being reliant on others.

When a child's duties as caregiver are managed so that the role as caregiver does not overshadow other aspects of his life, then the child may benefit from and even enjoy the responsibilities of caregiving. Ensuring that a child can still participate in activities with other children is critical in maintaining a healthy emotional balance for the child caregiver.

Unfortunately, a balanced caregiving routine does not always happen. A healthy caregiving relationship can quickly become a huge problem for a child—especially when the relationship is a child caregiving for his or her parent. Caregiving for a grandparent, sibling, or family member is one thing, but a child who is a caregiver for a parent is a very different situation with a much more complex dynamic.

Where Problems Start

When children are caregivers to their parent, an instant role reversal occurs in the relationship. If a child provides care for a parent on a short-term basis, say while a broken bone mends, a sense of teamwork can evolve. The child may gain a feeling of pride in his or her ability to contribute to the family unit. However, the longer the period of caregiving drags on, the more fragile the situation becomes.

The illness or disability of one parent creates for a child, a loss of that role the parent has always played in the child's life. Whether it is baking cookies together, playing video games, fishing trips or shopping at the mall, many things that a child may associate as part of the parent's function may no longer be possible.

Moreover, the loss of one parent from the 'parenting' role is just the beginning of the problem. Frequently, when one parent becomes seriously ill or disabled a child essentially loses both parents. The healthy parent must now step up his or her game, earning more money, assuming more responsibilities, and trying to be both the mom and the dad while keeping up with his or her own new role as a caregiving spouse.

What's Really Happening, By the Numbers

(From the report, *Young Caregivers in the U.S.*)

- Thirty-six percent of children who act as caregivers and are under the age of 11 report feeling as if no one loves them.

- Twenty-seven percent of children who act as caregivers have problems getting along with their teachers. This represents a fourteen percent increase over non-caregiving children.

- Twenty percent of caregiving children report that their responsibilities have caused them to miss school or miss an afterschool activity, while fifteen percent say caregiving has prevented them from doing homework.

The facts tell the story. Children as caregivers can work out beneficially for both the care recipient and the child . . . or it can be a disaster, leaving a child angry, resentful, hurt, sad, lonely, tired and overwhelmed by feelings of helplessness.

Here are some of the problem scenarios that can occur for children in the role of caregiver.

The Guilt-Burdened Caregiving Child

Helping someone during a time of recovery can be wearisome but it is almost always rewarding. Recovery means healing; it means success and progression in a forward direction. Because the patient is seeing improvement, his or her morale may falter, but will generally be encouraged, making him a pleasanter patient.

The caregiver also feels encouraged by seeing his or her efforts 'pay off'. But caregiving situations in which there is no progress yield frustration for both the care recipient and the caregiver.

When the patient does not visibly improve, it is hard for a caregiver of any age to feel heartened, but especially for a child who is more likely to be pragmatically looking for direct results from his or her actions. In this type of situation, feelings of failure as a caregiver and subsequent guilt for having failed often engulf the child.

The Weary Caregiving Child

Caregiving is exhausting for adults. For children, whose bodies must channel a great deal of energy into learning and growing, the demands and stress of caregiving often claim much-needed sleep and relaxation time from the child's life.

The American Academy of Sleep Medicine and the National Sleep Foundation suggest that younger elementary-age children need as much as ten to eleven hours of sleep each night and that older elementary-age children need nine to ten hours of sleep nightly. Lack of sufficient sleep in children has been linked to growth and development problems, irritability, obesity, inability to concentrate, and a variety of other health related or emotional conditions.

The Depressed Caregiving Child

This can be any caregiving child, even under the best of circumstances. The combination of physical weariness and the emotional complexities inherent in caregiving are enough to make even the strongest person feel sadness and for a child, the responsibilities of caregiving can become crushing. Changes in eating patterns, (consuming either less or more food than has been typical for the child) changes in sleep patterns, nail biting, bed-wetting, moodiness, withdrawal from family or friends, or school grades dropping noticeably are all signals that a child caregiver may be depressed.

The Compromised Caregiving Child

The compromised child is one whose role as caregiver should never have occurred in the first place. These children provide caregiving for themselves and sometimes their siblings, essentially running the household while their drug or alcohol using parent(s) indulge their addiction. Compromised caregiving children may also take on responsibilities like brewing coffee to help their parent's hangover, telephoning to offer excuses for the parent unable to get to work, or helping the parent dress and get out the door because the parent is unable to do so without assistance. A compromised caregiving child's responsibilities are out of both the child's control and the parent's. This is the one type of caregiving no child should ever be called upon to provide, yet is also one of the most difficult to identify and track because it involves conditions that are often hidden from others outside the home.

Everyone's Problem; Everyone's Responsibility

The children dealing with guilt, exhaustion, depression or the inappropriate actions of adults are the same children who show up in the statistics, feeling unloved, conflicting with authorities, missing school, and failing to complete assignments.

When caregiving gets out of balance in a child's life, all of the adults who surround him or her (whether they know the child personally or not) carry a measure of responsibility for rescuing that child. Neighbors, teachers, relatives outside the household, and the community at large must find ways to step up, give more, and create grown-up solutions to a very grown-up problem.

The burden of caregiving cannot be allowed to consume the life of even one child, much less the millions who are reportedly at risk. The solution is less about money and technology and far more about adults reaching out in acts of love and caring to people and families in need.

Children cannot control the timeline of how much is asked of them as a caregiver and they cannot control any of the emotional variables of the caregiving situation. The bottom line for children as caregivers is that they may be able to care for the physical needs of another person, even their own parent, *but they cannot provide caregiving for themselves.*

"Being deeply loved by someone gives you strength,
while loving someone deeply gives you courage."

Lao Tzu

4 FINDING THE BALANCE: LOVE, LUST, AND CAREGIVING

If the goal is to infuse your caregiving relationships with more love and your loving relationships with more caring, you have to be able to recognize which relationships are based on love, which ones are based on caring, and in some cases, which ones are based only on lust. Love is inherently selfless. Lust is inherently selfish. Caregiving can be either, neither, or both.

Ironically, selflessness is not always a positive quality, as it can take on a life of its own and transcend into martyrdom. Selfishness can, under the appropriate conditions, actually be a good quality to have to the degree that is promotes self-love, self-care and offers some protection against the tendency for selflessness to take on unhealthy proportions.

Balance in all things, especially all things caregiving, is important. But one of the biggest challenges of achieving balance is first being able to identify the types of relationships in which you engage.

Help, I've Fallen and I Can't Get Up

From time to time, you'll hear people make the interesting distinction between being 'in love' with someone and loving them. Being in love is reasonably easy to recognize, right? Racing heartbeat, sweaty palms, a sense of strange anxiety … or wait … maybe that is the description of someone experiencing a heart attack.

In a way, falling in love actually *is* a type of heart attack. People rarely walk steadily and surely into love. They inevitably plunge, plummet or fall. The result of any fall is that eventually you hit bottom. You then must pick yourself up and continue onward, hopefully having gained greater wisdom and prudence.

The human heart has amazing capacities for love of all types, measured both in depth by loving one person deeply and in breadth by loving many people. Losing a loved one in your life is painful, traumatic and may leave scars that are forever tender because you felt the love deeply.

Yet because of the expansive capability of the heart to love, we are able to move forward in our lives even after traumatic loss. Other loves may or may not be of same category as the love lost, but they still fill the very human need for experiencing loving relationships.

A grieving father loses a child—a heartbreaking situation—yet because that parent has other love relationships in life, his wife, other children, his parents, or even a career that he loves, he is able to rebalance his life and move past his grief. He does not stop missing or mourning the lost child, but the resilience of the human heart enables him to both love in multiples and love repeatedly.

Parents give birth to their first child, loving that child passionately, but they then go on to love each son or daughter born in later years equally as dearly. The human heart is apparently knitted together from a wonderfully stretchy and expansive fabric. People heal from lost love, broken engagements and even from the pain of divorce or the death of a person they love because they have other love-based relationships that help fill their lives.

Fortunately, replacement relationships do not need to be an apple for apple exchange. You can replace a lost romantic love with a new love interest, a puppy or a renewed enthusiasm for working with disadvantaged children. One relationship will not be the same as the other, nor will it fill the same spaces in your heart. No one would suggest that a Shih Tzu brings to your life the same dimensions as did the love of another person. Yet as any passionate pet owner will confirm, loving that pet is a relationship of love given and love returned and because of this, is tremendously fulfilling to the heart in ways we all desperately need.

Getting Back Up Again: Your Love Relationships

By the time you reach adulthood, you probably have realized that love is very tricky stuff. A combination of luck, timing and effort allows those who fall in love to transition from their head-over-heels experience to a loving relationship that is long lasting, fulfilling and stable. Getting the factors of luck, timing and effort into balance, and then keeping them that way, is part of what makes the whole business so precarious and unpredictable.

In the falling in love stage of a relationship, your heart attack may come at you from many angles and in unexpected ways. Depending upon the actions or lack of actions by the object of your adoration, you may feel euphoric one moment and crushed the next. Within the same heartbeat, you can be courageous beyond all measure and as vulnerable as a kitten. Moreover, as risky as falling in love tends to be, most people go out into the world looking for the fall.

In contrast, your Shih Tzu is a relatively safe love relationship because your dog will nearly always love you back. Barring illness or accident, your dog can be in your life to love you for many years—but only if you are also willing to be your dog's caregiver, providing those things a domestic dog needs but cannot provide for itself.

In a simplistic way, romantic love that we manage to stabilize (you can't keep falling forever) and then sustain, is much like that loving relationship with your Shih Tzu. When you get past the puppy love of thinking everything your beloved does is adorable, if you can start seeing him or her as having needs you must observe, respond to, and honor, and if you step up to those responsibilities, then you may very well find yourself to be the recipient of bountiful levels of love, loyalty and adulation.

All relationships come with a falling in love stage, not just the romantic ones. You meet a new friend and you're thrilled by how you enjoy his or her company and how much the two of you have in common. Over time, you realize that your new friend has plenty of quirks and needs. Whether you choose to fulfill some of those needs while that friend is also filling needs in your life determines if the friendship grows or even survives. And if either of you becomes too demanding on the other, overly selfish in your requests, or too accommodating and selfless, the friendship gets out of balance and either fades into the distance or implodes in some type of ugly moment or unpleasant event.

Even your love for an experience, such as golfing or pottery making, has a honeymoon period. You love the sound of the ball dropping in the hole or the feel of the clay in your hands. You can't wait to pick out the hottest new clubs or have your garage rewired to accommodate a kiln. After a while, you begin to discover that you probably won't become a scratch golfer in one season (maybe never) and that hitting buckets of balls on the range is not only sweaty business but gives you painful blisters on your hands. The new potter learns through trial and effort that throwing a well-balanced vase on a pottery wheel is amazingly difficult and even the most carefully crafted pottery may crack or explode during the process of firing, leaving the potter with only broken shards of the bowl that might have been.

Love-only or lust-only relationships are never really in balance. They tend to survive just about as long as you (or the other party involved) need or want them to last. At a certain point, one of you inevitably chooses to add caregiving to the mix or chooses to let the relationship decline. You determine by your action or lack of action, which direction you take after the fall. You decide whether to stop mincing your words and feelings about loving someone, being in love or caring for them, and start focusing instead on achieving balance.

The love-based relationships that survive in your life do so because you commit to enriching them with caregiving ... you choose to add caregiving to one side of the scale and loving to the other side with the focused desire to create balance in the relationship and balance in your life.

Your Personal Caregiver List

You will find it helpful to create a personal inventory of your caregiving and care receiving relationships. Most people are shocked to realize what a large number of relationships they have in which they give or receive care. When you make a Personal Caregiver List, you begin to see more clearly where love is missing from a caregiving relationship and where caregiving is in short supply in a loving relationship.

On your list, identify the people for whom you provide care, the people who provide care for you and those relationships where there is mutual caregiving and care receiving. After you have done this, you can start bringing out-of-balance relationships into better equilibrium by adding more care or more love as needed.

5 PROFESSIONAL CAREGIVERS

Jen will do it. Call on Jen.

There are always people in every group and every family who see to it that things get done. These people are professional caregivers—not to be confused with members of a caregiving profession.

Jen may be an accountant at the department store where she works, but if she is the person who reminds others of deadlines, fills out forms so they don't have to, double-checks the audit so her boss will look good to his supervisor, and volunteers to work weekends to get the stockholder's report finished, then Jen is a caregiver. She is doing her job and is doing part of the job of other people because she serves as their reminder, alarm clock, safety net, and crutch.

Jen may like her role as a professional caregiver or she may resent it. Either way, she is likely to be trapped in it unless she is (or becomes) highly aware of what patterns and imbalances have put her in this role and continue to keep her there.

Jen's position can be crippling or it may be empowering. Just like any other caregiver, she can find herself overwhelmed if she does not take responsible measures to keep her life in balance. Sacrificially caring for others is like running your car without ever changing or replenishing your oil. You can do it, and for a while it may carry you and others where you need to go, but sooner or later that engine will seize and you will be left waiting for a tow truck to rescue you and facing an expensive repair bill to pay.

Professional Caregiver, Is it You?

One of the biggest challenges for professional caregivers is that they often do not realize the role(s) they have assumed and because they don't recognize that they are overextended, they wind up stretched to the breaking point and wondering how it happened to them.

On the following pagers are ten questions to ask yourself to help you determine if you are a professional caregiver.

1. I remind my boss or coworkers of upcoming deadlines and responsibilities, even when it is not my deadline or I have already done my part.

a.) frequently   b.) occasionally   c.) never

2. I listen to other people's problems even when doing so puts me behind on my own schedule.

a.) frequently   b.) occasionally   c.) never

3. People ask me for rides to the airport, to work when their car is in the shop, or in other similar situations.

a.) frequently   b.) occasionally   c.) never

4. I do non-work related favors for people with whom I work.

a.) frequently   b.) occasionally   c.) never

5. I do favors for people who do not do favors for me.

a.) frequently   b.) occasionally   c.) never

6. I spend at least one night per week or one day on the weekend helping a friend, family member or coworker with their project, need or responsibility.

a.) frequently   b.) occasionally   c.) never

7. I have finished my children's homework or school project for them when they were sick, had a schedule conflict, or I thought they needed sleep.

a.) frequently   b.) occasionally   c.) never

8. My boss expects things of me that he or she does not expect from my co-workers in similar jobs.

a.) frequently   b.) occasionally   c.) never

9. I skip recreational or social activities because I am involved in helping someone else with a need or challenge.

a.) frequently   b.) occasionally   c.) never

10. I have stayed up all night or at least into the early morning hours at least once in the last two months because I was helping someone who is not a member of my immediate family.

a.) frequently   b.) occasionally   c.)never

Now tally your score.

If you have four or more a's or a combined total of six a's and b's, you are a professional caregiver.

Your acts of caregiving may take place in your family, the workplace, within your community, your neighborhood, or in clubs and civic organizations. Caregiving comes as second nature to many professional caregivers, meaning they take on caregiving responsibilities without realizing they have done anything out of the ordinary.

Professional caregivers often justify their actions by saying that they are merely making things easier on themselves in the long run by shouldering part of someone else's load. Being a professional caregiver is not inherently a good or bad quality in a person. Instead, the value or detriment of being a professional caregiver comes in how you manage and internalize the role.

The Professional Caregiver as Martyr

Professional caregivers who know they are in the role and who do not really like being there may actually be professional caregiving *martyrs*. They 'care give,' but they resent doing it.

They may have found themselves stuck in their role as professional caregiver because they are too timid to speak up and voice their desire not to be the caregiver for their boss, co-workers, spouse or others. They may be frightened of losing a job, losing favor with their employer, losing the love of their spouse or partner, the security of a marriage or relationship, or simply losing their social niche. Plagued by concerns such as the potential of losing their job or whether their friends will stop liking them if they stop acting as the mother hen or father goose, professional caregiving martyrs continue to take on responsibilities they would rather not have.

In the language of addiction, caregiving martyrs are enablers. Their willingness to take on someone else's responsibility prevents the other person from being responsible for his or her own load.

When a co-worker calls and says, "Would you email me the project file, again?" they are really telling you that even though you have sent them the work once, they either didn't bother to keep up with it or they don't want to bother to now search their past emails to find it. Instead, they want you to search through your emails and when you find it, as they know you will (because you keep up with everything) they expect you to send it to them for the second, third or perhaps fourth time.

Anyone is happy to forward a file occasionally to someone who has genuinely lost a document, but we all know people who expect others to serve as their personal filing system, resending files, documents, spreadsheets or other items for which they are too lazy to search out themselves. And the demands on caregiving martyrs rarely stop with searching for lost files.

The most dangerous aspect of being a caregiving martyr is that this caregiver is angry both at the people who expect too much of him and at himself for letting it happen. When people are angry with themselves, they rarely take the steps necessary to take care of their own needs as a care provider. In reality, they may do just the opposite and engage in self-destructive behaviors such as overeating, failing to get adequate sleep and exercise, and other actions that reflect their discontentment with their role.

The Professional Caregiver in Control

While some professional caregivers take on unwanted caregiving tasks because they don't know how to get out of them, others do so because they relish the sense of control that comes with their role. Knowing that people depend on you and need you to fill in the gaps in their life can be a heady and empowering feeling, resulting in a professional caregiver in control.

The caregiver in control takes on tasks and responsibilities because, to this type of professional caregiver, it feels good to know that other people can't get by without assistance from them. These caregivers may not realize that they are offering their caregiving efforts in order to embed themselves in the lives and routines of others. They often do not realize that they are trying to make themselves indispensible so that others actually 'owe' them for their caregiving actions. Control driven caregivers feel a surge or high from knowing how much other people need them.

The Well-Balanced Professional Caregiver

Before you decide that being a professional caregiver is a sign of full-blown mental instability, let's look at when this type of caregiver is a positive and beneficial role to play.

Well-balanced professional caregivers recognize that they are carrying others with their acts of caregiving. They extend themselves to these people not out of fear or in order to ingratiate others to them, but because they genuinely enjoy the acts of service they are providing. Their personality may be such that organizing, directing, rescuing and assisting are interesting and fulfilling tasks, especially when caregiving for someone with a genuine need and not just for someone who is too lazy to care for himself. Professional caregiving, when offered with love and kept in balance, never damages either the caregiver or the care recipient.

At times, each of us actually needs to give sacrificially of ourselves to others—it is part of what fulfills us emotionally at a very cerebral level. But each person's first and foremost caregiving responsibility is to take care of him or herself. As rewarding and as necessary as caregiving for others may be, it always involves carrying part of someone else's load, and for that, you must keep up your own stamina and conditioning.

"One word frees us of all the weight and pain of life;
That word is love."

Sophocles

6 CAREGIVING PROFESSIONS

Chapter 2 included a lengthy list of caregivers who might be in a child's life and it's a safe bet that the caregiver list for most adults would be at least as long. If you made your personal caregiver list when you were reading Chapter 4, it is probably, in fact, only a partial list.

Caregivers include all of the people you recognize as being in that role and an endless number of other people you may never previously have acknowledged as caregivers.

Some caregivers touch your life for a moment, others perhaps for many, many years. You interact with certain caregivers because you choose to and with others because you hire or contract them to provide you with some type of caregiving service. There are even caregivers in your life, such as law enforcement officers, fire fighters, or paramedics who are there because you pay for their services via taxes or assessed fees.

Merriam-Webster Dictionary OnLine[ii] records 1966 as the date the word caregiver first entered into the dictionary; *Merriam Webster's Collegiate Dictionary*[iii] dates the word only to 1975. Logic tells us that caregiving has existed at least since the day one caveman or cavewoman offered food or shelter to another. The fact that the word didn't find its way formally into the modern English language until the twentieth century speaks volumes.

No wonder people act as caregivers (both paid caregivers and those who serve voluntarily) without realizing they are in the role or understanding that their own survival hinges on how well they can provide caregiving for themselves during the process of caregiving for others. How can we culturally understand what it means to be a caregiver, when as recently as thirty to forty years ago, we didn't even have a word for it?

Our vagueness in understanding caregiving explains a lot about why people we do acknowledge as being in caregiving professions typically receive support systems so flimsy that that even the most devoted among them is likely to be functioning with some degree of burnout at any given time in their career. And to further complicate matters, we persist in compartmentalizing the experiences of caregiving and loving as if the two are disconnected.

The result of our collective confusion about caregivers, the caregiving professions, and caregiving roles in general is a series of problems that have far-reaching personal, social, and economic consequences for all of us.

Caregiving Careers on the Road to Burnout

Do you remember your last hospital experience, either as a patient or as someone connected to a patient, and how impressed you were that a well-rested, focused, and enthusiastic nurse was always around when you needed one?

No, of course you don't.

Burnout in healthcare occupations is at record high levels, just as it is in law enforcement, teaching, and dozens of caregiving-based service professions. Budget cutbacks to personnel have turned much of the already over-extended workforce into a weary and beleaguered group of professionals, spread too thin and trying to carry too heavy a load.

Because employers typically do not (and oftentimes economically cannot) offer preventative measures to provide more care for the caregivers in their employ, quality of service declines, turnover rates soar, and incidence of employee error, illness and absenteeism reaches startling numbers.

The solution? Well, that can be complicated and slow in evolving.

Even Those in Caregiving Professions are Baffled

Former First Lady Rosalynn Carter was a child caregiver to her father and her grandfather. She grew up watching her mother in the role as primary caregiver to both of these family members, a responsibility her mother carried for roughly forty years.

As is the situation with many caregivers, Rosalynn Carter did not see herself as a caregiver. It wasn't, she explains, until she became involved with developing the Rosalynn Carter Institute's caregiving program that she realized she too was a caregiver. Through her commitment to help her aging mother, even though she and her mother were not living in the same household, Rosalynn Carter was acting as her mother's caregiver.

Her compassion, fueled by her personal experiences, led Georgia's First Lady, who later became America's First Lady, to become a strong advocate on both the state and federal level for better mental healthcare services, greater protection of senior citizens, and more support of all whose life circumstances put them in the position of caregiver.

In her book, *Helping Yourself Help Others*[iv] Rosalynn Carter writes about Virginia Schiaffino, who at the time the book was written was a clinical social worker and the executive director of the National Federation of Interfaith Volunteer Caregivers. Virginia reported that among her adult siblings were, "…two social workers, a physician, a college professor, and a sister who worked for the leading law firm in New York City."

Despite this surfeit of professional knowledge, the siblings were, "baffled by the system," when it came to providing caregiving for their aging parents. Even turning to their church, they found little guidance in dealing with their family's situation.

As an author, Rosalynn Carter was making the point that caregiving in America is such a misunderstood mess that a family of five successful adult children—several in caregiving related fields by profession—found themselves bewildered and left to ask, "What do we do" when faced with a process as natural and as inevitable as aging parents.

Sadly, although some thirty years have passed since this former First Lady took up the cause, the situation has only worsened. Many nations, America among them, face the dual-whammy of caregivers by profession on the brink of crisis with countless unpaid caregivers already over the brink.

We may finally have a word in our language for those who provide caregiving, but obviously, we don't have a plan for executing the practice of caregiving and safeguarding the needs of those in caregiving professions. Caregiving in all its forms is as baffling as it ever was.

What Role Does Love Play Here?

People in caregiving professions are innately at risk. In addition to their professional duties to provide care to others, they no doubt have their personal list of people for whom they provide care.

We need our caregivers; we need them desperately for all the physical tasks they perform, services they render, and the psychological security blanket they afford us. So if not out of concern for the quality of their lives, we should at least be motivated by concern for our own lives and seek to ensure that those in caregiving professions are nurtured and cared for themselves.

To the degree that governments and business can financially afford it, we must find ways to 'legislate' love. This means looking seriously at vacation time, healthcare benefits, training and extended training opportunities, overtime requirements, staffing levels, and the combination of issues that contribute to overwork and stress for those in caregiving professions.

In a world obsessed with connecting via social media, where if Facebook were a country it would be larger than India in population, we need to transfer some of that time and energy into connecting via social support instead of merely social network. Volunteer in ways that offer hardworking, overworked caregiving professionals some relief. Raise awareness (and raise money) to support efforts that will directly improve the quality of life for a professional caregiver. Share your skills. If you have a service or product that will make life easier for people who work in caregiving professions—spread it around! And lastly, in a small suggestion that carries huge benefits, become a nicer person. As the Roman poet and philosopher, Ovid, advised more than two thousand years ago, "If you want to be loved, be lovable."

Putting forward even a small measure of grace and forbearance helps lighten the load for everyone. When you inject kindness, patience, and compassion into all of your interactions with caregiving professionals and all of your interactions as a caregiver, you defuse tension. You aren't shortening the length of someone's workday, but you are helping to make that day pass more smoothly.

By an act as simple as choosing not to be cranky and aggressive during rush hour traffic, you decrease the likelihood that you or others will be involved in an accident. You potentially (and exponentially) reduce the impact a traffic accident could have on an entire family, the added workload it might create for emergency responders and medical providers, and the short or long term caregiving needs it might create.

By taking a moment to pass on a smile, pleasant word, or a helping hand to another person, you defuse situations in which errors, accidents, outbursts, and poor decision-making are likely to occur. You demonstrate for others what grace and forbearance look like in daily life and inspire them to mirror your words and deeds as they go forward. Even children (especially children) pick up on your contagious goodwill, carrying it into the classroom and onto the playground.

The question is not one of whether love has a place in caregiving professions; it is only one of how we can foster greater feelings of love and caring into these professions. If you are in a caregiving vocation, imparting love into your caregiving responsibilities helps both those for whom you provide care and your fellow caregivers. Significantly, imparting love into your caregiving helps you.

Love the people with whom you interact, love the privilege of serving them, and love yourself so that you become a better and more loving caregiver in your role. You and your own loved ones will benefit as much or more than will the people you serve.

On the other side of the situation, none of us as care recipients is required to love our doctor, police officer or hairdresser, although they are worthy at least of our love as fellow human beings. But because we love ourselves and our families, acting in loving and caring ways toward the caregivers who look out for us, increases the chances of us receiving thorough and thought-driven care.

"Don't wait until everything is just right. It will never be perfect. There will always be challenges, obstacles, and less than perfect conditions. So what. Get started now."

Mark Victor Hansen

7 CAREGIVER BY DEFAULT

Sometimes you seem to get stuck in the role of caregiver. You walk into it, back into it, inherit it, or like Wile E. Coyote, a safe lands on your head and when you pull your nose up out of the sand, you find a giant weight planted firmly on top of you. You are a caregiver by default.

Caregiving by default comes loaded with internal conflict and is one of the most challenging caregiving roles you can assume. Yet like any other type of caregiving, it comes in all forms and many degrees, some clearly more stressful than others.

Consider these two examples of caregivers by default, each very different from the other.

The Marriage that Couldn't End

Anthony and Helen had spent more than twenty years in a marriage that had been emotionally unfulfilling almost from the beginning, but neither was ever comfortable with the idea of divorce. They lived separate lives underneath one roof, connected only by the two children born in the early years of the marriage.

After many discontented years together, life seemed to be turning in a better direction for them. Five years ago, Helen returned to fulltime work at an insurance agency owned by her brother. Nervous at first, she quickly found that she loved her job and that it gave her a new sense of purpose and self worth. During her third year, she was promoted into a management position that further boosted her financial situation and her self-esteem.

Anthony was in a very different place in his life. After teaching high school English for many years, he longed to use his skills in a different way. With their daughter married and their son in the Navy, Helen and Anthony now each had their own plans— hers involved renting a small apartment downtown to be closer to her work, while his would take him to the Dominican Republic to teach in a one-room rural school.

And then the safe fell.

While driving to work one April morning, Helen was involved in a serious three-car accident. Surprised she even survived the ambulance trip to the hospital; doctors were even more surprised many weeks later when they were able to send her home. But the hardest part lay ahead.

Helen faced months of rigorous physical therapy, speech therapy, doctors visits, and at least two, possibly three, more surgeries. Even then, it was doubtful she would ever be able to return to work or even live independently.

Although she and Anthony had long been 'emotionally divorced,' he felt that morally he could not leave her now. In the time it took the delivery van to crash into her car, sending it spinning into the path of oncoming traffic, Helen's bright future and all of Anthony's anticipated life plans shattered into a million fragmented pieces.

Congratulations, You've Been Promoted to Caregiver

In comparison to Helen and Anthony's story, Wanda's is far less tragic, yet Wanda, too, is a caregiver by default.

Wanda started working for a small advertising and design company almost immediately after finishing a two-year program at the community college. The entry-level pay she drew was tough to live on and the hours were extremely long as she tried to turn out the very best design work possible for each client no matter how short the turnaround or how many last-minute changes they requested.

After seven years that felt at least twice that long, Wanda learned that her company's creative director was leaving for a position in Atlanta, a larger market with more opportunities. Wanda was thrilled to be offered her former boss's job, a position that came with both expanded responsibilities and appreciably better pay.

What Wanda didn't anticipate was that her new job would put her in such an uncomfortable position dealing with the company's CEO. Not only was he old-school in his approach to advertising, causing her to push uncomfortably hard for ideas and practices she believed in, but he was extremely dependent upon whoever was in this job to cover many of his own professional and personal responsibilities.

Wanda needed this promotion. She had justifiably earned it and her family immediately began to benefit by the considerable pay increase that came with it. Besides, she recognized that there was no going back. Her old job was already filled.

Wanda could look for a new job, but realistically she knew the combination of a tight economy and her unwillingness to relocate to another area made it highly unlikely that she could find any employment that paid as well as her new position paid her. Wanda had been in her new role only a few weeks when she realized her promotion included the position of creative director *and* the role of caregiver for the CEO. The safe that fell on Wanda fell slowly, but there was no way she could have seen it coming.

People become caregivers by default every day. Some people eventually find a way out of their situation while others seem to remain stuck there forever. Anthony was long past loving Helen, yet felt responsible because of the many years they had spent together. Wanda began her new job with no feelings one way or the other about the company's CEO but quickly grew to dislike him.

What Anthony and Wanda shared in common was that each of them was in a caregiving relationship that did not involve feeling love for the person receiving the care. They believed they had no loving emotions with which to fuel themselves for their daily role, only a nagging sense of obligation that neither of them could shake.

Yet even caregivers by default make choices. Anthony was taking care of his wife because given the circumstances, (which he certainly had not chosen) he then *did choose* to change his life plans and provide care for Helen. Helen could have gone into a nursing home where she would have received competent care. The couple's daughter would also have agreed to take care of Helen. But Anthony was not comfortable with the impersonal, institutional care he felt Helen might receive in a nursing home nor did he like the way putting Helen in a nursing home made him feel about himself. Maybe some of the same feelings of obligation that had kept him in a loveless marriage for so many years now also stopped him from walking away from Helen after her accident. At the same time, Anthony didn't want his daughter and son-in-law, a young couple just getting started, to bear the responsibility of providing Helen's daily care.

While Anthony was a kind and thoughtful caregiver to Helen, and probably one of the best people for the role, he didn't take it on because Helen or anyone else forced him into it. He became a caregiver in order to reconcile his own feelings of responsibility. Anthony was addressing the needs of his personal moral compass.

Anthony's decision was a not an easy one and there were plenty of times he questioned it. But his discomfort with feelings about 'what kind of man' would leave his wife in a nursing home was greater than his disappointment over not accepting the job in the one-room schoolhouse.

You may hear people describe a caregiver by default situation as a circumstance that does not give them any choices. What they really mean (even though they may not realize it) is that they don't like the choices a situation offers. Life however, rarely loads us up with lots of win-win-win-options. With almost every decision we make, there are things gained and things lost.

Wanda recognized she had choices. She could continue in her job, carrying her workload and most of her boss's workload. She could leave the job for another one that would likely come with a considerable cut in pay and perhaps even take her away from the design work she loved.

Despite her limited formal education, Wanda thought her professional experience might allow her to land a comparable job if she was in a bigger city, where there were more opportunities. But relocating would mean her husband had to give up a job he enjoyed in hopes of finding employment in a new locale.

Relocation would also put them in the undesirable position of selling their home in a depressed real estate market and it would mean moving away from Wanda's parents who provided her with childcare that was loving, convenient, and free.

… Or Wanda could wait. She could hope that her boss would retire sooner rather than later and that when he did, he would hire someone to run the company who was more pleasant and less demanding than he was.

Wanda, like Anthony, had choices. And both found that much of their frustration stemmed from the fact that neither had choices that did not involve doing something they did not want to do. Caregivers by default are stuck in their roles when they do not see a way out or they are uncomfortable or unwilling to go with any of their options.

Does Love Have a Place Here?

Caregiving by default relationships can appear to be caregiving without love. While these relationships are typically lacking the sense of love a caregiver would feel for the care recipient, when you look more closely, you see that love in one form or another, is usually present.

Anthony may not have felt love for Helen, but he cared enough about her in some way to feel concern over the quality of care she would be receiving. He clearly felt love for his daughter, in that he would rather assume Helen's caregiving than leave his daughter and her husband to shoulder that responsibility.

And very importantly, Anthony loved himself, which is not *in any way* a bad thing. Anthony recognized that there were certain responsibilities or actions he needed to fulfill in order to feel good about himself as a person. He also knew that for him, leaving Helen's care to others was not an option with which he would ever be comfortable.

Perhaps over time, the intimacy of his caregiving relationship with Helen would cause him to feel loving feelings about her once again. Helen was after all, a person he had loved (or thought he loved) enough at one time to have married.

Wanda, on the other hand, is not likely ever to feel loving feelings toward her boss. But her decision to stay in the job is also love based. Wanda loves the work she does as the company's creative director. She loves her husband who is happy in a job that is fulfilling to him. She loves the fact that her increased salary helps her family enjoy more security and that by remaining near her parents she knows that they can continue as caregiving grandparents, a role they truly enjoy while her children are blessed with the most loving caregivers possible.

Wanda's choice also involves loving herself. She does not want to give up the advancement she has worked hard to gain; she is willing to put up with a difficult boss in order to have the other fulfillments that come with the job. Wanda has made a choice, and while it may not be ideal, it is loaded with love of many kinds.

Self-Care for the Caregiver Makes a Difference

Caregivers by default may not be able to change their situation, but they can improve how they *experience* their situation. As surprising as it may sound, they can honor their role as caregivers. This begins with being honest with themselves about why they are caregivers and being proud of their decision.

Every day good things—great things—happen to other people because of the actions of caregivers by default. Caregivers who open their eyes (and their hearts) will begin to see the blessings and benefits they are bringing to others and can savor the positive, reaffirming feelings this gives.

Anthony was not only improving Helen's life, he was improving the lives of his son, his daughter, and his son-in-law by taking on Helen's caregiving himself. Other members of Helen's family, including her parents and her siblings, along with her friends and her former co-workers were grateful to see the person they loved in the hands of a committed caregiver.

Wanda's caregiving actions benefited her family but also improved the daily lives of other people who interfaced with her boss, such as his family members and the other employees at the ad agency. Because of her willingness to shoulder so many of her boss's responsibilities, the company continued to thrive, and thirteen families were impacted by the employment it provided.

Caregivers by default can re-frame their situation. They can improve their experience by moving away from a victim mentality. Being a caregiver, whether on purpose or by default, is a reason to feel pride and to find joy in the fact that your actions improve the lives of others.

Five Small Changes that Really Help

No situation is impossible. Some are tough, some are jammed against the wall with their complexities but all have potential for at least small improvements. As overwhelming as a caregiving circumstance may seem, there *are* ways to change it, even if the change is only incremental or temporary.

When you are in a caregiving situation you resent, you are on a dangerous path. Any tiny bit of relief you gain is worth going after. You never know which effort will turn out to be the critical difference-maker that enables you to hang on and hang in there. Taking action to improve your situation is empowering and essential.

Here are five things you can do to make being a caregiver an easier experience. Try them. The harder ones are easier to do than they may seem. The easy ones are more effective than you might imagine.

1.) Just Say "Yes"

Being in a caregiving situation, especially when it is one you don't want to be in, can be off-putting and daunting. You may find yourself surrounded by negatives, focusing on all the things you can't do because of your circumstances and all the things your care recipient can't (or sometimes won't) do for himself.

Life turns into a series of negatives strung together in an endless chain. "Can't, "don't," and "won't" may become a huge part of your vocabulary and sooner or later a part of your thought process. You begin to assume that your care recipient cannot do certain things, sometimes without ever giving him the opportunity to try. You may also begin to feel that you can't do certain things such as find someone to help you, work in time for exercise and relaxation, or reclaim even a portion of your life.

One 'no' piles on top of the next and before you realize what has happened, you are living behind a giant wall of negativity that you may come to believe is insurmountable. Letting 'yes' back in to your life is a process you may have to relearn but 'yes-lessons' are all around you once you start to seek them.

Look to draw insights from nature, letting the universe teach you its message. A winter day can feel extremely bleak with a gray and barren landscape marked by the silhouettes of leafless trees, yet as dismal as it may seem, this is not a dead landscape. The trees are living and they will again burst forth with green leaves and fragrant blossoms. The ground is still fertile and new life will return. You can be growing inside even during the darkest times.

Change, improvements, or assistance won't show up in your life (or if it does you may fail to recognize it) if you are not open to receiving positive experiences. Be willing to try things that don't always make sense on the surface.

Open your mind to new ideas, new people and the new opportunities they bring with them. Visualize the wall of 'no' crumbling and a stream of possibilities flooding through. Even a landscape brimming with the potential for growth and new life must have sunshine and nourishment in order to make it happen. Don't block out your own sunshine.

2.) Don't Gamble

When you are scampering round and round on the caregiver's treadmill it is easy to hope that 'one day' your life will return to normal. *Don't bet on it!*

Putting your life on hold while you wait for an event to happen at some undetermined future date will come back to bite you.

What are you waiting for—an overly demanding boss to retire? The person for whom you are caregiving to die? A selfish spouse to get hit by a truck?

Okay, that's a pretty morose way to live. When you are in a caregiving situation that you do not want to be in and see no way to get out of, you have to find ways to live more of your life in the moment and to make those moments more worthwhile. Yes, this sounds like a simplification, but even if it is, *it is your only alternative!*

Caregivers often speculate that they can neglect their own need for rest, healthcare, exercise, social engagement, and relaxation while they take care of the needs of others. Too many times caregivers put their life on hold, literally waiting for someone else to die, only to find that the plan backfires.

The caregiver dies before the care recipient does … or the care recipient dies, but the caregiver finds that his or her own health has become so poor that the things he has been waiting to do are no longer possible.

Neglected friends move on, life changes, and the world doesn't stop while you live as a sacrificial caregiver. A gambling caregiver too often finds that he or she has given up so much of his life, there is little left to which to return when the caregiving demands end.

3) Lighten Your Load

The tasks, demands, responsibilities, and burdens you experience as a caregiver sometimes feel like an enormous weight, but a generalized sense of being overwhelmed is hard to address and hard to improve. You must be able to name a problem before you can solve it or even improve it. Any attempt to manage or alleviate your complaints begins with first acknowledging them.

Plan a few minutes of quiet time when you can think about and then list every complaint you have about your role as caregiver. Use 3 x 5 file cards and write only one complaint or problem on each card. List small gripes as well as the big ones. Your list might include things such as (1.) tiredness from the long hours, (2.) feeling like you never have time to read/watch football/soak in the tub, etc. (3) missing social activities you would like to be enjoying, or anything else that you resent or dislike about your role in caring for someone else.

There are no right or wrong items to include on the list. Your list will be private, so go ahead and tell it the way you really feel it is.

When you are finished, bundle your cards together with a rubber band. They may make a small stack or a large pile, but no matter how many cards you have, they are a tactile representation of the burdens, resentments and anger you are carrying with you each day. Your cards represent a load you need to lighten.

As often as you can, (daily is suggested) go to your cards and select one that you can choose to relinquish for the day. If you can select more than one, all the better, but at least find a way to give up one burden or one responsibility for that day.

When you have selected your item, physically remove the card from the stack, separating it from the other cards. You need to see a concrete action that demonstrates your intent; you need to see the card move from one side of the desk to the other or from the 'complaints' pocket of your jeans to your 'relief' pocket.

Perhaps you will have a friend, relative, member of your church or community agency that can provide a meal to the person for whom you are responsible. If you can get help with meals one or two days a week—take it. If you can get help with meals every day—seize the opportunity. And if you only get one person to cover you for one meal—accept it with appreciation and relief that for today that card is one you can remove from the pile.

The odds of you resolving all of your complaints are low (remember, the caregiving gambler rarely sees the payoff he is holding out for), but the chance to relieve yourself of even one complaint is worth going after. Set aside only one problem each day and then think of your load as 365 times lighter this year than it was last year.

4.) Find Something to Celebrate

In the U.S. there are eleven recognized federal holidays. In case you have been so busy caregiving that you have forgotten, they are: New Year's Day, Martin Luther King's birthday, Inauguration Day, Washington's birthday (unofficially known as President's Day), Memorial Day, Independence Day, Labor Day, Columbus Day, Veterans Day, Thanksgiving Day and Christmas.

Now let's expand this list with some additional holidays that the federal government does not formally recognize. To your holiday list add: Mardi Gras, Super Bowl Sunday, Groundhog Day, Valentine's Day, Saint Patrick's Day, April Fool's Day, Good Friday, Easter, Earth Day, Arbor Day, Cinco de Mayo, Mother's Day, Flag Day, Father's Day, Patriot Day, Constitution Day, Rosh Hashanah, Yom Kippur, Leif Erikson Day, Halloween, Election Day, Hanukkah, Christmas Eve and Kwanzaa.

These two lists add up to nearly forty holidays, most of which you probably ignore and do not celebrate. If you were also to add in family birthdays, graduations, anniversaries, job promotions, the cat's birthday, engagements, weddings and certain divorces, you could realistically come up with perhaps fifty or more holidays you currently may be overlooking

If some of the holidays on these lists don't fit your lifestyle or your personal convictions, pick out days that do. Make a plan to celebrate the day you bought your new car, the release of a new book/movie/video game, March Madness, the World Series, the Stanley Cup, the first daffodil each spring, the first watermelon each summer or the last orange leaf of autumn.

If you don't like holidays from your own country, pick those that are celebrated elsewhere—the point is, choose holidays, commit to them, mark them on your calendar and then acknowledge them. Your list does not have to be logical to anyone else; it only has to make a small space of happiness for you.

Unlike the traditional approach to holidays that often calls for more preparation and expense than fun, make it a requirement for the holidays on your personal list to be celebrations that are mindlessly easy to implement. A fresh flower by your kitchen sink or on your work desk, a cupcake, gourmet coffee, lunch with a friend, a massage or an extra thirty minutes reading the sports page—celebrations don't have to come with a brass band and streamers.

For a celebration to give you a lift it can be as brief as a five-minute experience and as simple as pausing to enjoy every note of your favorite song, but in order for it to work, you have carve out that tiny space in your life for it to exist. When you do this, you are sending a message to yourself that your life is still connected to the moment and is worthy of celebration. Every time you break down a small part of the seemingly impenetrable walls of your caregiving situation, you mark a huge personal victory.

5.) Be Flexible

Being a caregiver may seem as if it is all about the care recipient. But in many ways, it is all about you, as caregiver.

The person for whom you provide caregiving may never become easier to help. Unless your caregiving situation happens to involve a patient who is healing or a child who is maturing, your care recipient is likely to become more difficult with time. You, and only you, can direct the quality of your life as a caregiver. The more you keep the path rigid and uneventful, the more difficult the experience becomes.

Caregiving is not an endless journey; although it is a road filled with twists, turns, potholes, and unexpected delays. But the scenery can be beautiful along the way. You will meet interesting people, you will travel farther than you expected and you likely will reach a destination that you could not have reached otherwise.

Raise your head, enjoy the view from the window whenever possible, get out and stretch your legs at regular intervals, don't forget to stop for food, bathroom breaks and fuel. The journey can turn out to be the ride of a lifetime, if you open yourself to the possibilities ahead.

Caregiving by ~~Default~~ *Selection*

Think back to the first sentence in this chapter, "Sometimes you seem to get stuck with the role of caregiver." What if caregivers could replace the perspective of being stuck with the thought that they were selected for their role as caregiver?

If you can believe in God, angels, fate, or just an overall sense that there is a greater order and purpose in our lives, then perhaps you can begin to see yourself as chosen to be in your caregiving role. Acknowledging that at this time, no one in the entire world can fill this role as well as you do, can lead you to a new perspective and a different outlook. Seeing yourself as 'chosen' can become the critical turning point that allows the healing power of love to rise to the surface in your caregiving situation.

When your caregiving burden feels too heavy, step back, look at yourself through the eyes of the world—through the eyes of the one for whom you provide care. You will see a person who is strong and tall; who is rich with the gifts of giving, caring, and compassion. Step into those shoes, because that caregiver is you.

Unknown

8 LOVING AWAY THE BARRIERS

Barriers to giving care and giving love crop up in many unexpected ways. Some are created by the environment, others by the person receiving the attention, and surprisingly, many are created by the person giving the care and the love. You've heard the expression about people who just can't get out of their own way? ...This can be the case with caregivers.

Barriers a Care/Love Giver Might Create

Let go of fear.

Good advice in almost all situations. Fear 'of' is inevitably more traumatic and more paralyzing than whatever it is you are dreading.

Historically the word 'fear' most frequently described those things or events that led to an emotional reaction of fright, as in, "My fears are big dogs, lightning, and speaking in front of large groups." But over time, the word has become much more about the emotion than the event, which is really unfortunate. An angry dog may bite you, but your own fear will prevent you from visiting friends who have dogs, or enjoying a walk in the park or around the block.

As a caregiver, fear creeps in when you are hesitant about saying or doing the 'wrong' thing. The worst result from this is rarely that you do or say the inappropriate thing, but more often, that you do or say nothing at all. Nothingness is one of the most depressing and detrimental emotions any of us face. The emptiness created by another person's failure to speak or to act can be especially damaging to people who are already dealing with challenges of aging, loneliness, loss of independence, or the pain and trauma of illness or injury.

Within reason, any action you take or statement you make is a better option than doing nothing. Naturally, when you are caregiving to someone who is seriously ill, dying, or emotionally unstable, you feel pressure to 'get it right'. Your self-created anxiety however, only makes things more difficult for you and for your care recipient. Yielding to this anxiety causes you to miss opportunities for which there may not be a second chance.

Conscious thought and past experiences can actually become barriers to your capabilities as a caregiver. Instead of filtering your thoughts based on what has happened to you previously, honor the moment you are in now. If the person you provide care to seems to need or want something that is not in sync with his or her past preferences, don't let that history guide your decision making. Think with your head, but act with your heart.

Preconceived ideas not only kill the moment, they abort the future that the moment might hold. Sometimes we wrestle with our problems or our concerns for so long that wrestling begins to feel normal. Barriers begin to look like the walls of home instead of like the obstacles to be torn down, that they really are. Simple is a good thing. Different may actually be your new normal. And new may turn out to be the best place you've ever been.

As a caregiver, strive to be intrepid. Ask, offer, suggest, reach out and initiate. Your courage will be appreciated and even contagious. Your willingness to try to move through barriers will be a powerful resource for you and for the care recipient.

Taking Barriers Down Through Small but Meaningful Acts

Responsibility for giving care doesn't include responsibility for giving a cure. It may not even include responsibility for the things you expect it to at all. Sometimes, the greatest gifts a caregiver has to offer require the smallest efforts.

Giving hope is a big gift you can give in a small package; especially when you are giving to a care recipient who has lost hope himself. As a caregiver, look for opportunities to 'stand in the gap' letting your care recipient lean on you and borrow your hope. As mother and caregiver, Janet Lynn Mitchell told her chronically ill daughter:

"Honey, today you're tired and you've lost all hope. Today, you can rest in my arms and let me hope for you. You can be assured that my hope is endless and so is my love[v]."

Care recipients may have many physical needs, but their emotional needs are likely just as great. A young cancer patient tells the story of how hard she tried to maintain a positive and upbeat attitude about her treatment. To this single mother, overwhelmed by her situation, it seemed that people were constantly sharing stories with her about their friend/cousin/co-worker who had beaten cancer by laughing at reruns of *I Love Lucy* or *Saturday Night Live*.

The fact that her health was not improving despite what she believed was her best effort to keep a positive attitude made her feel worse—it was as if she not only was seriously ill, but somehow was contributing to her own deteriorating health. "If only," she thought, "I could laugh harder, maintain a better attitude, or do something that other cancer patients have done that I am not successfully doing …"

Her relief came through the words of an astute doctor who joined her treatment team at the point when all previous treatments had failed. Sensing her anxiety, he told her, "You can go off duty now. Eli Lilly (the pharmaceutical company) and I will take it from here. You did not cause your body to develop this cancer and you are not responsible for the cure."

With these insightful words, this caregiving physician took down a barrier for his seriously ill patient. One cannot help but feel that the weight he lifted from her shoulders helped to contribute–along with his medical expertise and the right pharmaceuticals–to her remarkable recovery.

Talk to caregivers—*listen to caregivers.* Over and over you will hear them voice the same stories—the same concerns. They need more hours in the day. They need more help. And above all else, they need people who will help them in specific ways, whatever those ways may be.

In the case of the young mother battling cancer, her needs were twofold. She needed the friends who showed up at her house, scooped up her children and her dirty laundry, and said, "Rest, I'll be back tomorrow with your children and your clean laundry." They didn't ask, which would have given her a chance to put up a barrier and politely refuse; they just provided the care they could see was needed.

For this cancer patient, the doctor who reframed her thoughts about her responsibilities and the friends who served up love and laundry to her children were great caregivers. But as she struggled with the traumas of treatment and the uncertainties of what might lie ahead for a mother, not yet thirty, with an absentee-ex-husband and two young children, she also needed a caregiver to listen to her thoughts.

Today, healthy and feeling far removed from her life or death battle with a disease that kills some 7.6 million people[vi] worldwide each year; she recalls that most people didn't want to hear her fears.

In her own words, she explains, "In retrospect, I realize I made many people uncomfortable about their own mortality.

"I was young, people around me saw me as very healthy, and suddenly my life turned upside-down and I was facing a type of cancer where the odds were really against me.

"Everyone wanted to help and I deeply appreciated the help and needed all that they did for me. But I only had one friend who was really comfortable with letting me talk. And for months after my recovery, I still felt a strong need to share the frightening experience with someone.

"I wasn't looking for answers. But I needed to tell my story—to put the experience into words—repeating parts of it over and over, as a way to bring the cancer-monster out of the dark.

"Daniel listened. He nodded sympathetically, occasionally asking a caring question—it was exactly what I needed. I understood that most people didn't want to hear the details of my illness, its treatment or my fears. They didn't want me to talk about the experience; they wanted me to put it in the past and I don't blame them for that. But I will forever be grateful to Dan for listening to me. Cancer is so invasive in your life. Even after your body is rid of it, it takes time to purge it from your spirit.

"Today, I hear about someone with the same cancer I had, and I think, 'oh yes, I had that too,' but I have so completely gotten past it—with Dan's help—that it doesn't define me anymore and I actually have to stop and recall the fact that it ever happened to me at all."

Some caregivers provide medical treatment and healing. Others offer clean laundry and childcare. And then, there are some caregivers whose most important role is simply to listen.

Who Are You, Anyway?

Chapter 7 looked at the importance of tearing down the wall of 'no' and negatives in a caregiver's life. Care recipients deal with that wall as well. The experiences of a care recipient can leave a person feeling special and valued by others or it can result in him or her feeling as if he has lost all autonomy and the right to make his own decisions. Self-identity is interwoven with many aspects of a person's independence.

Being a care recipient always involves relinquishing areas of control. Medical professionals may be making critical decisions about a care recipient's health. Family members may be deciding upon issues of lifestyle or finance. Needing care not only makes a person vulnerable to others in new and unsettling ways, but brings a type of change that can erode a person's identity.

When you ask people to tell you about themselves, they frequently begin by telling you about the work they do, their hobbies, their travel, or even their favorite sports.

"Hello, my name is Lilly and I am a schoolteacher who likes to spend my summers camping, gardening and reading mystery novels. Oh yes, and I am a big Denver Broncos fan, too."

Think about how many times you have heard people give this type of description about themselves to a group or to new people they are meeting. Now think about how often a person in need of care has to compromise some or all of the types of things that were on Lilly's list. Without the 'things' you do, it is easy to lose track of who you really are.

A care recipient's natural resistance to give up freedoms, independence, and identity may feel like a barrier. Recognize it for what it is: a protective wall. Instead of caregiving through actions that may take away freedoms or minimize a person's sense of self, try caregiving in ways that build up and even restore these feelings for the care recipient.

The American Medical Association's Guide to Home Caregiving explains, "Do not confuse doing with caring. Recognize that your loved one will benefit from remaining as independent as possible for as long as possible. Resist the urge to do everything for him or her, and encourage your loved one to participate in his or her daily care routine[vii]."

The acts of caregiving you provide should, as much as possible, protect and encourage the self-identity of your care recipient. Whether you are providing care as a spouse, a parent, to an ill or elderly family member or as a routine part of your job, every time you demonstrate respect for the care recipient's dignity, identity and independence, you tear down (or prevent) barriers. You eliminate the need for self-protective walls. Your respectful caregiving strengthens and empowers your care recipient. Most importantly, it enriches the lives of both the giver and the recipient because it is caregiving that is heavily fortified with love.

Stop Taking all the Credit (*Blame*)

You really aren't the person for whom you provide care. When you provide caregiving for someone, not only is he or she at risk of losing his identity—so are you.

If your caregiving puts you in the situation of caring for a person who is compromised in some capacity, that person may act or respond in ways that just don't fit the cultural norms. Or he or she may need assistance that draws attention to the situation in ways that you find embarrassing.

Okay, time to separate your identities. You can only go through life responsible for your own deeds, actions and those of your minor children. How a care recipient may act does not reflect on you nearly as much as you may feel that it does.

Most people will not judge you by the actions of others for whom you provide care. In the off chance that they do, ignore them; as Mother Theresa said, "If you judge people, you do not have time to love them."

Judgmental people are just working on their own issues of love and caring; step back from them as much as possible, you have your own caregiving on which to focus.

Love the people for whom you provide caregiving inasmuch as you are able. Protect them in the ways that you can, including those times that you can graciously intercede to protect them from their own actions. But let go of all the things you cannot change.

In life, we are not our drunken spouse, our senile parent, or our best friend who has just embarrassed us at an elegant restaurant. You are not condemned in a case of guilt by association, unless you choose to condemn yourself.

You may not like what the people for whom you provide caregiving do or say. Yet remember that you love them for the person they are (or were) when they are not under the influence of pain, drugs, narcotics, stress, dementia, or disease. Focusing on your love for them goes a long way to preventing barriers built out of your own embarrassment.

Is Caregiving Different for Men than it is for Women?

The answer to this is 'no' … and 'yes'.

Men do not feel less deeply than women feel, nor is a man's capacity for caregiving any less than that of a woman. However, some women may arrive on the scene better prepared to act as a caregiver than do some men.

At an early age, little girls start wrapping baby dolls, kittens and unwilling younger siblings in blankets. They rock them, burp them whether they need it or not and stroll them around in pink plastic baby carriages. They are practicing caregiving and rehearsing a role. However, there are just as many little girls and little boys who never nurture dolls and kittens, but instead carry a frog in their pocket or keep a snake in a jar. They too, are practicing the role of caregiver.

Whether it is cultural, genetic or a random fact of the universe, most caregivers are women, typically between the ages of 45 and 64[viii]. Do women wind up in this role because they volunteer for it? Because of default? Or because many men—feeling unprepared to deal with it—back away from these responsibilities?

Marc Silver is the author of *Breast Cancer Husband*, and himself the caregiver in a role he describes as becoming, "… a member of a club I really didn't want to join."

In his insightful book about his role as caregiver, patient advocate, moral support—and oh yes, *husband*—he tells his own story and the stories of other men who have been there to share the experience with and care give to their own wife as she fought the battle of a lifetime. Silver writes:

"…when your wife is fighting a life-threatening disease, you want to be on top of your game. The problem is, you've never been on the playing field before. … Most guys are complete novices when it comes to this caregiving thing.[ix]"

Maybe the reason caregiving feels less than natural to some men is as simple as the fact that they aren't as accustomed as women may be to being in those shoes. That's okay, this does not have to be a barrier. Caregiving fortunately seems to come with a lot of effective on-the-job training. You can catch on and catch up very quickly!

Men or women who find themselves thrust into the role of caregiver, or even evolving into this role, handle it best if they can learn to roll with the punches as much as possible. Listen, do what you know how to do, learn how to do a few new things, take instruction, ask questions, forgive yourself and the person for whom you are caregiving, and very importantly, **_don't try to solve everything._**

Think of caregiving like one of those math tests you once took in school. You may not get the right answer, but that's okay. You get lots of credit for showing your work. You'll still pass the test.

Simplify Everyone's Life

Some barriers are easier to deal with than are others. Removing physical barriers that may be unsafe or impede the mobility of a care recipient improves his or her life and the life of the caregiver. When the environment is clean, simple and clutter-free, everybody's routine is easier.

Not all such barriers are physical; some are functional barriers, such as not having an easy-to-read calendar handy. Even if your caregiving does not involve someone who is ill or elderly, the following simple steps just make sense for everyone:

- Keep a calendar, making it easy for everyone involved to keep track of appointments, schedules, and reminders.

- Always have at least one clock that is easy to read, easy to set and has a battery backup.

- Clear out furniture that isn't needed, serves no function and just takes up space and requires dusting.

- Purge clutter. Doing this simple task serves to alleviate a great deal of anxiety for anyone who lives or functions within the space.

- Reposition corded phones, lamps, throw rugs and anything else that could contribute to a fall, or make an area harder to navigate.

- Use adequate lighting as well as night-lights.

- Use a nonslip mat in the bathroom.

- Be sure that some things are readily accessible for anyone receiving care or anyone providing it including batteries, a flashlight, a phone that is easy to use, a toilet plunger, and a fire extinguisher.

- Keep a back-up supply of drinking water, basic medications, paper towels, disposable plates and utensils, toilet tissue, waterless hand cleaner, and non-perishable foods such as peanut butter, dried fruit, nuts and canned tuna. No matter where you live, an unexpected power outage, severe weather, or a transportation challenge could put you in the position of fending for yourself. A little preparation goes a long way to improve emergencies.

Look at this list (the one you almost skipped reading because you already know this 'stuff'). If we all know it, why don't we consistently do it?

Whether you are caregiving for others or just as an act of caregiving for yourself, *make life easier!* Address basic creature comforts so that they don't add to the stress and problems you already deal with in life. At the risk of sounding like your grandmother the profound truth is: *an ounce of prevention is worth a pound of cure.*

Troublesome Barriers for Caregivers

While removing some barriers is as easy as relocating the chair everyone keeps tripping over, other barriers, particularly the kind that seem to exist primarily in your head, can take a real effort.

When you are feeling weary and overloaded already, it is often hard to imagine fighting one more fight. These types of psychological barriers include problems such as not taking care of yourself because you rationalize that you don't have time to look after the needs of your own mental and physical health.

If you need motivation to help move you past psychological barriers, then consider the needs of the person or people for whom you provide care. Put yourself in their shoes. When you board a plane, do you want your pilot to be overworked and exhausted? Before your surgery, do you want your surgeon to be dealing with a case of the flu, forcing him or herself to come in and remove your appendix when he or she really should be home in bed? Or how about the mechanic who fixes the brakes on your car ... is it okay with you if he or she is so depressed and despondent that he is just trying to get through the day, with little concern for the quality of service he provides?

As the authors of *Caring for the Caregiver*, a book developed by Parke-Davis to assist caregivers of Alzheimer's patients, remind us: "You as the caregiver *do* have an obligation to yourself. But you are also important to the patient."[x]

Pat Samples, with Diane and Marvin Larsen, has developed a twelve-step program for caregivers explained in their book, *Self-Care for Caregivers, a Twelve-Step Approach*. Reminding us, "... the first person we are responsible for in this life is ourselves," their book challenges caregivers to become highly self-analytical and examine how they are handling the responsibility of self-care.

The next chapter you will read is titled, "Love Thy Self." In some ways it is the most important chapter in this book as it deals with ways you, as a caregiver, can protect, respect, nurture and heal—not your care recipients—but your care recipients' lifeline.

--The lifeline that is YOU!

"The greatest degree of inner tranquility comes from the development of love and compassion. The more we care for the happiness of others, the greater is our own sense of well-being."

Tenzin Gyatso, the 14th Dalai Lama

9 LOVE THY SELF

Set aside the theory, the emotion, and what your instinct tells you about those things you do not have time to include in your caregiving efforts. Here are the facts about caregivers, with appreciation to the National Family Caregivers Association for much of this information:

- Nearly half of all of working caregivers report that an increase in caregiving expenses has caused them to use up all or most of their savings. Across the United States, caregiving families have median incomes more than fifteen percent lower than those of non-caregiving families.[xi]

- Female caregivers of persons with dementia are, on average, nearly four times more likely to develop the condition themselves than persons who don't have an affected partner; male caregivers are twelve times more likely.[xii]

- The stress of caregiving for someone with dementia impacts the caregiver's immune system for up to three years after the caregiving experience ends.[xiii]

- Between forty and seventy percent of family caregivers have "clinically significant symptoms of depression" with roughly one quarter of them being diagnosable as having major depression.[xiv]

- Family caregivers under extreme stress have been shown to age prematurely; reducing the caregiver's life expectancy by as much as ten years.[xv]

- Seventy-two percent of family caregivers report that they do not go to the doctor for their own health needs as often as they should.[xvi]

- Sixty-three percent of caregivers report poor eating habits.[xvii]

- Fifty-eight percent of caregivers indicate that their exercise habits have declined as compared to their exercise habits before they were caregivers.[xviii]

- Thirty-five percent of caregivers classify finding personal time for themselves as an unmet need.

Twenty-nine percent say managing emotional and physical stress is also an unmet need.[xix]

- When a wife is hospitalized, the husband's chances of dying within one month increase by thirty-five percent. When a husband is hospitalized, the wife's likelihood of dying within one month increases by forty-four percent.[xx]

Read enough? These statistics are not the whole story; they are only a faint rumbling from the avalanche of documented research and statistics linking the stress of caregiving to financial problems, depression, increases in many types of illness and decreased life expectancy for the caregiver. If it seems that the wellbeing of caregivers (and aren't we all caregivers to someone in life?) is hanging by a thread, then you are closer in your understanding of the situation than you may realize—although the thread a caregiver's life hangs by is actually more like a shoestring.

Dr. Elizabeth Blackburn is a distinguished biochemistry professor at the University of California San Francisco and recipient of the 2009 Nobel Prize in Medicine or Physiology, along with numerous noteworthy professional awards for her many years of research. As one of the world's leading researchers on the study of stress, aging and biochemical changes at the cellular level, Dr. Blackburn explains the scientific concept that she compares to a shoestring.

"Telomeres are the protective caps at the ends of chromosomes in cells. Chromosomes carry the genetic information … In my lab, we're finding that psychological stress actually ages cells, which can be seen when you measure the wearing down of the tips of the chromosomes, those telomeres … Telomeres are buffers. They are like the tips of shoelaces. If you lose the tips, the ends start fraying."[xxi]

Long twisting strands of your DNA, the very essence of everything that is you, are subject to literally unraveling in the presence of psychological stress. And when Dr. Blackburn and Dr. Elissa Epel, a psychologist who studies the effects of chronic stress, teamed together to study adults under stressful conditions, the subjects they selected were a control group of mothers with a normal, healthy child and a second group of mothers who each had a child with a chronic illness. That's right—when you want to study stress—pick caregivers as your subject.

The result of the research on the stressed caregivers showed that among the stressed group, the longer the mothers had been caring for their chronically ill child, the less telomerase (the enzyme that restores the telomeres when they become worn down) was present and the shorter the telomeres were. Dr. Blackburn saw these findings as further scientific proof of how something outside the body can affect the body's potential to repair itself. Not surprisingly, a later study of women who were primary caregivers for a partner with dementia yielded similar findings.

Caregiving, when managed and balanced in life, is rewarding and fulfilling. Left to spin out of balance, without love for the care recipient and love for yourself as the caregiver, caregiving can cost you your health, happiness and even your life.

Your Life, Your Choice

So, do you really love yourself enough to love yourself? Only you know the answer to this for sure. You will be a better caregiver for others in life if you commit to taking care of and loving yourself first.

Good intentions, like New Year's resolutions, are usually short-lived. Running shoes, a gym membership, a yoga class or trips to the organic food market are all great ideas, but despite an overload of messaging about these healthful options, the world is still filled with overweight, out-of-shape people who eat the wrong foods. Most of us don't want to be lectured to; we want to be inspired.

A change of attitude goes a long way to fostering a healthy and long-lasting change of heart. Instead of a grandiose plan to enrich your own life with more self-care, start with something much simpler: self-love.

"In life, you can never be too kind or too fair; everyone you meet is carrying a heavy load."

Brian Tracy

10 COMING FULL CIRCLE:

CAREGIVER AND CARE RECEIVER

Nationally known consultant and trainer, Maya Hennessey[xxii] stepped into the role of caregiver in the split second that followed a restaurant server turning to her and saying, "Excuse me, ma'am, your husband seems to have had a seizure."

From Maya's experience in caregiving for her late husband came her book, so appropriately titled, *If Only I'd Had This Caregiving Book*. Her approach to caregiving is distinctive, drawing from her professional skills in teaching and training others.

Using a system that has come to be known as Maya's Model, Hennessey puts the tool of Mind Mapping to work as, "… a creative method to extract solutions and enhance harmony between you, your To-Do List and your SSN (Social Support Network)."

The twelve-step approach identified in the book, *Self-Care for Caregivers,* offers another way to manage your role as caregiver without giving up your own health and sanity. Because it is patterned along the lines of other twelve-step programs, millions of people easily identify with its direction and can apply it in their lives.

In the book, *God's Heart—Your Hands,* author, counselor, and caregiver Laurie Zurinsky, provides day-by-day prayers and meditations based on Christian principles. Laurie shows how to draw strength from scripture and God's promise to love and strengthen His children. Laurie advises caregivers not to make important decisions in a F-O-G, what she calls decision-making based on **F**ear, **O**bligation, and **G**uilt. The only worthwhile motivator, she says, is love.[xxiii]

The similarities and the differences in Maya Hennessey's story and the strategies she explains in her book, and in the twelve-step approach to caregiving, or the scripture-based style of Laurie Zurinsky remind us that caregiving strategies, like caregiving situations, come in all sizes, degrees, and types. None of them of course, can be beneficial to you unless you are willing to try them.

Love, first and last, is your critical key. In order to incorporate love into your acts of caregiving and caregiving into your loving relationships you must be able to:

> 1.) Recognize that you are in a caregiving situation and your life will be changed by it.

2.) Embrace the changes of caregiving, which inevitably means you will stop doing or start doing something (probably a number of things) within your life patterns.

3.) Understand that as the measure of love you feel for others *and for yourself* increases, so will the quality of your caregiving experiences.

Perfecting the Imperfect Art of Caregiving

Even with its drawbacks and demands, caregiving is an unavoidable, inevitable, and totally desirable part of this life. Its desirability comes, in part, from the fact that absence of caregiving received or given means a deficit of relationships in your life.

A big empty void.

Why not make it a priority life goal to become the best caregiver possible? When you do, not only will those for whom you provide care benefit greatly, as will practically everyone who comes in contact with you, but you will also benefit in ways that will permeate every aspect of your life.

A wise father once counseled his twenty-six-year-old daughter, who was upset when it seemed to her as if all of her friends were falling in love and marching down the aisle. With insight and love, the father recommended that she stop thinking about finding Mr. Right and instead become very self-focused on becoming Mrs. Right. He was, in a sense, challenging her to love herself more.

He challenged her to become the best future wife a man could ever find, striving to grow in wisdom, spirit, self-discipline, knowledge, patience, determination, life-experience, and accomplishment. If she took this on as her objective, not only would she be distracted from her concerns over when or if she would marry, but she would actually be better preparing herself for whatever roles, as a single or a married woman, she might play in life.

Of course, during her pursuit of becoming the best possible bride, the appearance in her life of the best groom took care of itself. Profound wisdom from a loving parent and great advice that could be applied not only to finding romance, but to all of your life relationships.

Imagine how many fewer divorces there might be if husbands and wives began to focus, not on the failings and shortcomings of their spouse, but on how they could turn themselves into the best marriage partner possible?

Now carry this same strategy forward into all of your caregiving and loving relationships. What would it require of you to embark on the mission of reinventing yourself as the best and most loving caregiver ever?

First, you would have to recognize all of your caregiver roles and expand your caregiving outreach to both care recipients and other caregivers. You'd need to open yourself up to receiving the blessings of caregiving and to embracing the caregiving experience for all it can bring into your life.

Of course, you would need to let go of fear, indecision, inflexibility, guilt, anger, and a range of other paralytic emotions that benefit neither you nor those around you. But above all else, you would have no choice but to care for the caregiver, and love yourself more.

Becoming the best caregiver possible would require you to demonstrate responsibility for your own health, happiness, personal growth, prosperity, and security. You very simply, have to put the oxygen mask on your own face before you could help anyone else acquire oxygen of his or her own.

Everything You Need to Know, You Learned in Little League

Home runs win baseball games. But games are also won by good pitchers who stay alert and back up third and home; by outfielders who infield off fly balls; and by runners who remember to keep their eye on the base and not the ball. An endless number of small things come together in a big way to create a victory.

Being the best catcher, pitcher, or outfielder is never enough. Success is built by the contributions of a team even though some players will contribute only in small ways while others contribute significantly. In the rules of sportsmanship and success that we teach children—*"Don't try to do it all by yourself; don't hog the game, it will cost you the win."*

As elementary school children move from tee-ball to more advanced teams, they are excited as they realize that they can hit a ball that has been pitched toward them a much greater distance than they could hit that same ball when it was stationary and they were hitting it from a tee-ball stand. The laws of physics teach us that an object in motion moves further when acted upon than does a stationary object.

This is you, as a caregiver, a lover, a love giver, and a citizen of life. Stay in motion. Keep trying. Learn from your losses, remember to warm up first, reflect on how your efforts benefit the team, always take full advantage of the seventh inning stretch, and never try to carry the whole team on your back.

What? Perks for Caregivers?

Help sometimes comes not just in the form of others who offer time or assistance but in subtle ways that we can easily miss. When perks and benefits show up, *take them!*

One mother, whose adult child is disabled, says it took her years to learn to 'take advantage of the perks'. While reading a summons she had received for jury duty, she noticed that the fine print explained that in her county, certain extenuating circumstances could permit a person to be relieved of jury duty. One of the circumstances was being a fulltime care provider for a mentally or physically handicapped person.

Yes, she could have served jury duty; she had done so many times before. She could have hired a sitter to stay with her son or dropped him off to visit a friend or relative and gone on to serve her turn at jury duty. Doing so would not have been greatly more inconvenient for her than it is for most parents who must squeeze jury duty into their busy schedules. And although she had always coped with such challenges, here was one she could choose to eliminate. She had an out—a qualifying out. So she took it.

The busy, overextended caregiver, decided to relinquish her feelings of guilt. She then called the Office of the Clerk of Courts and told them that she qualified for this special jury duty exemption. Without questions or hassles, they took her off the jury duty list for that trial, and forever more.

Could she have made it to jury duty, and served what most people see as a civic responsibility? Sure, but her life has had plenty of other hardships from which there have been no option for reprieve. The hours she has spent in doctors' offices with her son, the cost of special classes, special schools, and a long list of other factors have been part of her challenge as a caregiver. The right to sidestep jury duty doesn't begin to offset her many years of struggling as caregiver to her child, but it is a small way to make her life easier. Time had taught this caregiver to accept any breaks that came her way—large or small—with appreciation and no feelings of remorse.

Part of the process of taking care of the caregiver includes learning to accept help and benefits whenever and wherever they are available. In every situation, inquire if there are special services that can help you in your role as caregiver. Don't be hesitant to ask or embarrassed to accept help when it is available.

Places You Can Turn for Help

A private nurse or around-the-clock aide is not in everyone's budget. Neither are many of the other services that could make it easier for you to deal with your responsibilities in giving care. But you never know where help may come from until you ask.

Here some of the resources to consider when you need assistance: Medicare and Medicaid, private insurance plans, state-funded healthcare, Veterans Affairs, CHAMPUS (the Civilian Health and Medical Program of the Uniformed Services), Worker's Compensation, community and volunteer groups, and some managed care plans.

At the end of this book you will find a resource list; pages and pages of places where you can turn for help and information. You'll also find the names of books and articles that may be beneficial to you in the role of caregiver or even in the role of care receiver. The best thing about the list is that it is not complete, nor will it ever be, as more and more resources become available each year.

With an aging population and medical advancements to keep all of us alive longer, we each face an increase in the number of ways and the duration of time for which we will need to give care and receive it ourselves. Prepare yourself. Practice your skills as a caregiver. Day by day, interaction by interaction, seek to infuse unlimited love into your acts of caring and boundless measures of care into your commitments of love.

There's a fine line between loving and caring. Be sure you cross it freely, deliberately, and often.

"When one door of happiness closes, another opens; but often we look so long at the closed door that we do not see the one which has opened for us."

Helen Keller

ABOUT THE AUTHORS

WENDY PACKER, a Registered Nurse, is a dynamic lecturer and workshop leader whose speaking engagements include hospital grand rounds, support groups and civic organizations. She is a teacher in the adult education arena as well as a R.N. Educator. Her nursing career spans decades working in hospitals, clinics, home care and doctor's offices. She has added to her professional training the skills of Certified Consulting Hypnotist and Reiki Master/Trainer. She speaks frequently on the importance of taking care of self as a caregiver and is the creator of a social network for caregivers in all caring roles.

Learn more at: www.hypnonurse.com
www.careforthecaring.ning.com
www.caregivingbook.wordpress.com

LINDA J. PARKER is a writer, ghostwriter, published author, book coach, and rearranger of words for businesses, nonprofits, and individuals with a dream, a need, or a vision. Her expertise includes conceptualization, messaging, and problem solving, including a focus on conversion-driven results, quality content, and SEO/SEM.

Visit: www.lindaparkerbooks.com or email her at: info@lindaparkerbooks.com

TO ORDER ADDITIONAL COPIES OF THIS BOOK, OR
TO BOOK WENDY PACKER FOR A SPEAKING
ENGAGEMENT OR WORKSHOP...

Wendy Packer is a Registered Nurse, Certified Consulting
Hypnotist, Reiki Master/Trainer.

Respected and acclaimed as a speaker for seminars, workshop
leader, and for group or one-on-one consultations, you can
contact Wendy at:

(914) 589-0655
Wendy@hypnonurse.com

www.hypnonurse.com
www.careforthecaring.ning.com
www.caregivingbook.wordpress.com

RESOURCES

The following books and resources either were researched in the course of writing *Are You In a Caregiving Relationship and Don't Know It?* or are sources the authors believe may be helpful to you as you seek to better understand life's fragile balance of loving and caring.

This list is limited in scope. Inclusion on this list is not an endorsement or recommendation, nor is omission from the list meant to imply that a resource does not provide a valuable service.

Many of the associations and organizations listed here need both donations and volunteers, and your help would be greatly welcomed.

A Dignified Life: the Best Friends Approach to Alzheimer's Care: a Guide for Family Caregivers, by Virginia Bell and David Troxel. Health Communication Press, Deerfield Beach, Florida ©2002

A Place for Mom. www.aplaceformom.com (877) 666-3239

AARP www.aarp.org 601 E Street, NW, Washington DC 20049 888-OUR-AARP (888-687-2277)

Adaptive Environments Center, Inc. www.adaptiveenvironments.org (617) 695-1225 New Name – The Institute for Human Centered Design (IHCD)

Administration on Aging www.aoa.gov (202) 619-0724

Alliance of Claims Assistance Professionals (a non-profit organization to help find assistance in processing insurance claims) www.claims.org Texas Office – (888) 394-5163 or Connecticut Office – (888) 394-5163

Alzheimer's Association www.alz.org (800) 272-3900

Alzheimer's Disease Education and Referral Center www.alzheimers.org/adear (800) 438-4380

American Academy of Medical Acupuncture www.medicalacupuncture.org (310) 364-0193

American Brain Tumor Association www.abta.org
(800) 886-2282

American Cancer Society www.cancer.org (800) 227-
2345

American Diabetes Association www.diabetes.org
(800) 342-2383

American Health Assistance Foundation
www.ahaf.org (800) 437-2423

American Macular Degeneration Foundation
www.macular.org (413) 268-7660 (888) 622-8527

American Stroke Association
www.strokeassociation.org (888) 478-7653

Associacion Nacional Pro Personas Mayores (National
Association for Hispanic Elderly) anppm.org
(626) 564-1988

B'nai B'rith www.bnaibrith.org (202) 857-6581 (senior
housing issues) (888) 388-4224 (travel and volunteer
programs)

Blindreaders Info www.blindreaders.info
webmaster@blindreaders.info

Brain Injury Association, www.biausa.org
(800) 444-6443

Breast Cancer Husband, book by Marc Silver. Rodale,
©2004

Canadian Caregiver Coalition www.ccc-ccan.ca
ccc@ccc-ccan.ca

Care for the Caregiving, book sponsored by Parker-
Davis, Warner-Lambert Company, ©1994

Care for the Caring www.careforthecaring.ning.com

Caregiver Network, Inc. www.caregiver.on.ca
(416) 323-1090

CaregiversUSA www.caregivers-usa.org
caregivingforyou.com (310) 450-0660

Caregiving Book blog
www.caregivingbook.wordpress.com

Caregiving Newsletter www.caregiver.com
(800) 829-2734

*Caregiving: The Spiritual Journey of Love, Loss and
Renewal*, by Beth Witrogen McLeod. Publisher: John
Wiley and Sons, Inc. NY, 1999

Carers Australia www.carersaustralia.com.au
(800) 242-636

Carers UK www.carersuk.org 0808-808-7777

Catholic Charities USA www.catholiccharitiesusa.org
(703) 549-1390

Center for Advocacy for the Rights and Interests of
the Elderly (CARIE) www.carie.org (215) 545-5728

Chicken Soup for the Caregiver's Soul book by Jack Canfield, Mark Victor Hansen, and LeAnn Thieman, Health Communications, Inc., Deerfield Beach, Fl. ©2004

Children of Aging Parents (CAPS) www.caps4caregivers.org (800) 227-7294

DOROT (Generations Helping) www.dorotusa.org 212-769-2850

Eldercare Locater www.eldercare.gov (800) 677-1116

Eldercare Guide and Information http://ecguide.info

ElderCare Online www.ec-online.net prisminnovations@gmail.org

Gold Violin (products for special needs) www.goldviolin.com (877) 648-8400

Guide to Home Caregiving, a book by the American Medical Association. John Wiley & Sons, New York, 2001

HypnoNurse www.hypnonurse.com

If Only I'd Had This Caregiving Book, book by Maya Hennessey. Author House, Bloomington, Indiana, ©2006

Large Print Books www.largeporintbooks.com

Lighthouse International www.lighthouse.org
(800) 829-0500

Macular Degeneration Foundation www.eyesight.org
(888) 633-3937

Meals on Wheels of America www.mowaa.org
(703) 548-5558

Medic Alert www.medicalert.org (888) 633-4298

Mr. Eldercare Online, For Families Dealing with Aging
Parents www.mreldercareonline.com

National Academy of Elder Law Attorneys, Inc. 655 N.
Alverson, Suite 108, Tucson, Arizona 85771
naela.org (703) 942-5711

National Asian Pacific Center on Aging
www.napca.org (206) 624-1221 or (800) 336-2722

National Association for Visually Handicapped
www.navh.org (212) 821-9497 (Now part of
Lighthouse International)

National Cancer Institute www.nci.nih.gov
(800) 422-6237 www.cancer.gov

National Council on Aging www.noca.org
(800) 677-1116

National Directory of US Home Care and Health Care
Service Providers www.seniormag.com

National Family Caregivers Association
www.thefamilycaregiver.org (800) 896-3650

National Federation of the Blind www.nfb.org
(410) 659-9314

National Hospice & Palliative Care Organization
(NHPCO) www.hospiceinfo.org (800) 658-8898

National Institute on Deafness and Other
Communication Disorders www.nidch.nih.gov
(800) 241-1044   (800) 241-1055 (TTY)

National Women's Health Network (202) 682-2640
www.nwhn.org

Self Help for Hard of Hearing People, Inc.
www.shhh.org (301) 657-2248

The Alzheimer's Store www.alzstore.com   (800) 752-
3238

The American Self-Help Clearinghouse
www.selfhelpgroups.org (800) 367-6274

The Arthritis Foundation www.arthritis.org
(800) 283-7800

*The Caregiver's Survival Handbook: How to Care for
Your Aging Parent Without Losing Yourself (*book) by
Alexis Abramson, Perigee Books, NY, 2004

The Comfort of Home, a book SERIES by Maria M
Meyer, Mary S. Mittleman, Cynthia Epstein, and Paula

Derr, Jon Caswell, Susan C. Imke, Mary E. Gilmartin, Kay Kendall, Jennifer Reese, Lucy Mathew, Jill Chang, and other authors. CareTrust Publications LLC, Portland, Oregon.

The Compassionate Friends
www.compassionatefriends.org (877) 969-0010

The Elder Care Survival Guide: How To Care For Elderly Parents Without Losing Your Money, Your Family or Your Mind, (book) by Martin R. Sabel
http://mreldercareonline.com/elder-care-survival-book

The Family Caregiver Alliance www.caregiver.org
(800) 445-8106 or (415) 434-3388

The National Alliance for Caregiving
www.caregiving.org

The National Chronic Pain Outreach Association
www.chronicpain.org (540) 862-9437

The National Guild of Hypnotists www.ngh.net

Today's Caregiver (magazine) www.caregiver.com
(800) 829-2734

Well Spouse Foundation www.wellspouse.org
(800) 838-0879

Young Caregivers in the U.S. (report) compiled by the NAC, the National Alliance for Caregiving and the United Hospital Fund, September 2005

"You cannot teach a man anything; you can only help him to find it within himself."

Galileo

ENDNOTES

[i] www.cdc.gov/nchs/fastats/divorce.htm, Fast Stats from the Center for Communicable Disease (CDC).

[ii] http://www.merriam-webster.com/dictionary/caregiver

[iii] Merriam Webster's Collegiate Dictionary® Tenth edition, USA. 1994.

[iv] Rosalynn Carter, Helping Yourself Help Others, Times Books, New York, ©1994.

[v] Janet Lynn Mitchell, "When All Hope is Lost", Chicken Soup for the Caregiver's Soul by Jack Canfield, Mark Victor Hansen, and LeAnn Thieman, Health Communications, Inc., Deerfield Beach, Fl. ©2004.

[vi] American Cancer Society, "Global Cancer Facts and Figures 2007"
http://www.cancer.org/downloads/STT/Global_Facts_and_Figures_2007_rev2.pdf

[vii] American Medical Association, Guide to Home Caregiving. John Wiley & Sons, New York, ©2001.

viii The Canadian Caregiver Coalition www.ccc-ccan.ca

ix Marc Silver, Breast Cancer Husband. Rodale, USA ©2004.

x Care for the Caregiving, sponsored by Parker-Davis, Warner-Lambert Company, ©1994. p. 15.

xi Evercare Survey of The Economic Downturn And Its Impact On Family Caregiving; National Alliance For Caregiving And Evercare. March 2009.

xii Research based on a 2010 study of over 1200 couples and published in the Journal of the American Geriatrics Society

xiii Drs. Janice-Kiecolt Glaser and Ronald Glaser, "Chronic stress and age-related increases in the proinflammatory cytokine IL-6." Proceedings of the National Academy of Sciences, June 30, 2003.

xiv MetLife Study of Working Caregivers and Employer Health Costs; National Alliance for Caregiving and MetLife Mature Market Institute. February 2010.

xv Elissa S. Epel, Dept of Psychiatry, University of California, SF, et al.

From the Proceedings of the National Academy of Sciences, Dec 7, 2004, Vol 101, No. 49.

[xvi] Evercare Study of Caregivers in Decline: A Close-Up Look at Health Risks of Caring for a Loved One. National Alliance for Caregiving and Evercare. 2006.

[xvii] Evercare Study of Caregivers in Decline: A Close-Up Look at Health Risks of Caring for a Loved One. National Alliance for Caregiving and Evercare. 2006.

[xviii] Evercare Study of Caregivers in Decline: A Close-Up Look at Health Risks of Caring for a Loved One. National Alliance for Caregiving and Evercare. 2006.

[xix] Caregiving in the U.S. Key Findings: 2004, National Alliance for Caregiving and AARP.

[xx] Nicholas D. Christakis, Professor, Healthcare Policy, Harvard Medical School, Boston and Suzanne Salamon, M.D., Associate Chief, Geriatric Psychiatry, Beth Israel Deaconess Hospital, Boston, New England Journal of Medicine, Feb. 16, 2006.

[xxi] Claudia Driefus, "Finding Clues to Aging in the Fraying Tips of Chromosomes," New York Times. July 3, 2007.

[xxii] Maya Hennessey, If Only I'd Had This Caregiving Book, Author House, Bloomington, Indiana, ©2006.

[xxiii] Laurie Zarinksy, God's Heart—Your Hands, Xulon Press, USA, 2004.

CPSIA information can be obtained
at www.ICGtesting.com
Printed in the USA
BVHW030827060121
597114BV00008B/76

9 781463 507497